CYBERSECURITY ESSENTIALS

FOR ENGINEERS

CYBERSECURITY ESSENTIALS FOR ENGINEERS

Parveen A.
Associate Professor,
Dept of CSE, Sathyabama Institute
of Science and Technology

S. Priya
Associate Professor,
Dept of CSE, Sathyabama Institute
of Science and Technology

KHANNA BOOK PUBLISHING CO. (P) Ltd.
4C/4344, Ansari Road, Darya Ganj,
New Delhi, India

Sathyabama Institute of Science and Technology
Jeppiaar Nagar, Rajiv Gandhi Salai,
Chennai, Tamilnadu, India

Dear Readers,

To prevent the piracy, this book is secured with HIGH SECURITY HOLOGRAM on the front title cover. In case you don't find the hologram on the front cover title, please write us to at contact@khannabooks.com or whatsapp us at +91-99109 09320 and avail special gift voucher for yourself.

Specimen of Hologram on front Cover title:

Moreover, there is a SPECIAL DISCOUNT COUPON for you with EVERY HOLOGRAM.

How to avail this SPECIAL DISCOUNT:

Step 1: Scratch the hologram
Step 2: Under the scratch area, your "coupon code" is available
Step 3: Logon to www.khannabooks.com
Step 4: Use your "coupon code" in the shopping cart and get your copy at a special discount
Step 5: Enjoy your reading!

Thanks,
Khanna Publishing House

ISBN: 978-93-55388-52-0

Cybersecurity Essentials For Engineers
by **Parveen A., S. Priya**

First Edition: 2025
Reprint: 2026

To view complete list of books, please scan the QR Code:

Published by:
Khanna Book Publishing Co. (P) Ltd.
CIN: U22110DL1998PTC095547

Visit us at: www.khannabooks.com
Write us at: contact@khannabooks.com

Printed in Bharat.

Preface

In a world of growing interdependencies, the role of cybersecurity is becoming more vital. As engineers and technology professionals, it is imperative to understand the complexities of cybersecurity to protect sensitive information and ensure the integrity and availability of systems and networks. This book on "Cybersecurity Essentials for Engineers" is designed to provide readers with the foundational knowledge and practical skills necessary to navigate this critical field.

Unit 1 establishes the groundwork by discussing the essential need for security in our digital world. It explores various security approaches, principles, and components crucial for balancing security with access. This unit emphasizes the importance of integrating security into the Software Development Life Cycle (SDLC) and highlights the roles of security professionals within organizations.

Whereas, Unit 2 examines the threats organizations face today. From intellectual property theft to sophisticated software attacks, this unit categorizes various threats and vulnerabilities that can arise from human error, inadequate policies, and technological failures. Understanding these threats is vital for developing effective defense strategies.

Unit 3 offers an overview of essential tools that safeguard systems. Covering firewalls, VPNs, intrusion detection systems, and access control mechanisms, this unit equips engineers with knowledge on how to implement these technologies effectively to protect remote connections and sensitive data.

While Unit 4 introduces key concepts in cryptology, including cipher methods and cryptographic algorithms. This unit discusses the significance of cryptographic tools in securing communications and protecting data integrity against potential attacks on cryptosystems.

Finally, Unit 5 focuses on the protocols that ensure secure data transmission over networks. By examining standards such as SSL, IPSEC, and various encryption methods, this unit provides engineers with a solid understanding of how to establish secure communication channels in their projects. As cyber threats continue to evolve in complexity and scale, this book aims to empower engineers with the knowledge needed to design secure systems and respond effectively to emerging challenges in cybersecurity. Through a blend of theoretical insights and practical applications, "Cybersecurity Essentials for Engineers" serves as an indispensable resource for anyone looking to enhance their expertise in this vital domain.

Contents

♦♦♦

1 UNIT

Introduction to Cybersecurity

RATIONALE

This book chapter, "Introduction To Cybersecurity," is designed to provide a foundational understanding of the field. It begins by establishing the critical "Need for Security" in our interconnected world, highlighting the real-world consequences of cyber breaches and underscoring the imperative for proactive measures. The chapter then transitions into the practical and theoretical underpinnings, exploring various "Security Approaches" that encompass preventative measures, detection/monitoring techniques, response/mitigation strategies, risk management, and recovery processes, all grounded in the core "Principles of Security," such as confidentiality, integrity, and availability. It further delves into the tangible "Components" of a cybersecurity system, like firewalls and antivirus software, while addressing the essential challenge of "Balancing Security & Access" to ensure usability and productivity alongside robust protection. Emphasizing proactive security, the chapter incorporates the "Software Development Life Cycle" and the "Security Systems Development Life Cycle," illustrating how security should be integrated into every phase of software creation. Finally, the chapter acknowledges the crucial human element, focusing on the roles and responsibilities of "Security Professionals and the Organization," stressing the importance of collaboration and shared responsibility for cybersecurity across the entire organization.

UNIT OUTCOMES

- **Understand Core Concepts:** Students will be able to define cybersecurity and explain its core principles of confidentiality, integrity, and availability.
- **Recognize Security Needs:** Students will be able to identify and articulate the reasons for security in various contexts, including personal, organizational, and national security.
- **Apply Security Approaches:** Students will be able to describe different cybersecurity approaches, such as prevention, detection, response, and mitigation, and how they contribute to a comprehensive security posture.
- **Analyze Security Components:** Students will be able to identify and describe the components of a cybersecurity system, including hardware, software, and human elements, and how they interact.
- **Integrate Security into SDLC:** Students will be able to explain the importance of integrating security considerations into the software development lifecycle (SDLC) and the security systems development lifecycle (SSDLC).

1.1 INTRODUCTION

Cybersecurity, or information technology security, is the practice of safeguarding computer systems, networks, and data from digital attacks, unauthorized access, and potential damage. This encompasses a wide range of strategies and technologies aimed at maintaining the confidentiality, integrity, and availability of information. In today's interconnected world, the increasing reliance on digital infrastructure and the digitization of personal and professional lives make cybersecurity more crucial than ever.

The core concepts of cybersecurity are built around protecting sensitive information and ensuring the smooth operation of digital infrastructure. These concepts include confidentiality, which ensures only authorized individuals can access sensitive information; integrity, which maintains the accuracy and reliability of data throughout its lifecycle; and availability, which guarantees that information and resources are accessible when needed. Authentication verifies user identities before granting access, authorization determines the permissible actions, and non-repudiation provides proof of data origin and delivery.

Effective cybersecurity is an ongoing process that requires constant vigilance, adaptation to emerging threats, and a proactive approach to security. It's not merely a technical issue but a fundamental requirement for protecting privacy, data, and infrastructure in an increasingly digital world. As cyber threats evolve and become more sophisticated, individuals, businesses, and governments must prioritize cybersecurity to safeguard their digital assets and maintain trust in digital systems.

1.2 NEED FOR SECURITY

The need for robust cybersecurity measures stems from the increasing reliance on digital infrastructure and the exponential growth of data in modern life. Security is vital to protect sensitive personal information, such as social security numbers and financial data, preventing identity theft, fraud, and personal harm. Protecting corporate data, including proprietary information and customer records, is essential for maintaining competitive advantage, customer trust, and legal compliance. Equally crucial is safeguarding government information related to defense, intelligence, and public safety to uphold national security.

Financial security is another key area where cybersecurity plays a critical role. Cyberattacks like ransomware, phishing, and fraud can lead to significant financial losses for individuals, businesses, and governments. Maintaining the stability and integrity of financial systems, including banking, stock exchanges, and payment gateways, is vital for overall economic stability. Cybersecurity also ensures operational continuity by protecting business operations and critical infrastructure from disruptions.

In addition to data and financial security, cybersecurity is essential for protecting intellectual property, ensuring legal and regulatory compliance, safeguarding privacy, and ensuring national security. By adhering to data protection laws, cybersecurity helps avoid legal penalties, fines, and lawsuits. Protecting individual and corporate privacy is vital for maintaining trust and security in digital interactions and communications, while safeguarding defense systems and critical infrastructure ensures national security against cyber warfare and espionage.

1.3 SECURITY APPROACHES

Cybersecurity employs a wide range of strategies, technologies, and methodologies to protect systems, networks, and data from cyber threats. These approaches encompass preventive measures, detection and monitoring, response and mitigation, mitigation and risk management, recovery, and awareness and training. Each of these plays a vital role in forming a comprehensive security posture.

Preventive measures include access control through role-based access control (RBAC) and multi-factor authentication (MFA), encryption using techniques like AES and TLS, and network security measures such as firewalls and intrusion prevention systems (IPS). Detection and monitoring involve intrusion detection systems (IDS) that use signature-based and anomaly based detection, along with security information and event management (SIEM) for log management and real-time monitoring.

Response and mitigation strategies include incident response plans (IRP) and dedicated incident response teams, along with disaster recovery plans (DRP) and business continuity plans (BCP). Mitigation and risk management involve risk assessment through threat modeling and vulnerability assessment, and penetration testing through ethical hacking and Red Team/Blue Team exercises. Recovery includes data backup and restoration with regular backups and secure storage, and post-incident analysis through root cause analysis and lessons learned. Finally, awareness and training are vital, featuring security training programs for employees and the establishment of security policies and procedures.

1.4 PRINCIPLES OF SECURITY

Cybersecurity rests on a set of fundamental principles designed to protect the integrity, confidentiality, and availability of information systems and data. These principles provide a framework for developing and implementing robust security strategies. They serve as the guiding lights for ensuring that security measures are effective and aligned with the goals of protecting digital assets.

Confidentiality ensures that sensitive information is accessible only to authorized individuals, using techniques such as encryption, access controls, data masking, and tokenization. Integrity involves maintaining the accuracy and reliability of data throughout its lifecycle, employing hash functions, digital signatures, checksums, and version control. Availability ensures that information and resources are accessible to authorized users when needed, with redundancy, load balancing, backup and recovery, and disaster recovery planning.

Authentication verifies the identity of users and devices before granting access, employing passwords, biometrics, multi-factor authentication (MFA), and token-based authentication. Authorization determines what an authenticated user or system is allowed to do, utilizing role-based access control (RBAC). Non-repudiation ensures that a party in a communication cannot deny the authenticity of their actions or data, providing proof of origin and integrity through digital signatures and detailed audit logs.

1.5 COMPONENTS OF A CYBERSECURITY SYSTEM

A comprehensive cybersecurity system consists of a range of hardware and software components working together to protect digital assets. These components include firewalls, antivirus software, intrusion detection systems, and various access control mechanisms. Hardware components, such as firewalls and routers, are essential for creating a secure network perimeter and controlling traffic flow.

Software components, including antivirus software, intrusion detection systems (IDS), and security information and event management (SIEM) systems, provide the tools needed to detect, analyze, and respond to security incidents. Endpoint protection platforms (EPP) safeguard individual devices, while data loss prevention (DLP) solutions prevent sensitive data from leaving the organization's control. The interaction between hardware and software is crucial for creating a robust and layered defense. The components of Cyber Security is as shown in figure 1.1.

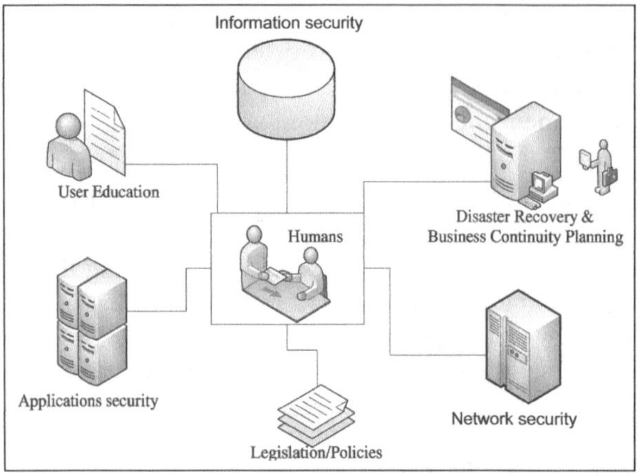

Figure 1.1: *Components of Cybersecurity*

Effective cybersecurity also requires understanding how these components work together to provide a layered security approach. Firewalls form the first line of defense, while IDS and SIEM systems monitor for suspicious activity. Access control mechanisms limit access to resources based on user roles and permissions. User education and training complement these technical measures, empowering users to recognize and avoid potential threats.

1.6 BALANCING SECURITY & ACCESS

Balancing security and access is a critical challenge in cybersecurity, requiring a delicate trade-off between protecting systems and data and ensuring usability and productivity. Overly restrictive security measures can hinder efficiency and create frustration for users, while lax security can expose systems to unacceptable levels of risk. Finding the right balance is essential for creating effective and sustainable security policies.

The need to balance security and access arises from the tension between protecting sensitive information and enabling authorized users to perform their job functions. Implementing strong authentication measures, such as multi-factor authentication, and access controls can improve security but may also add complexity and inconvenience for users. Encryption protects data but can also impact performance.

Strategies for finding the right balance include implementing risk-based security policies, tailoring security measures to the specific needs and risk profiles of different systems and data. User education and awareness are crucial for empowering users to understand security risks and adopt secure behaviors without compromising productivity. Regular reviews and adjustments to security policies are necessary to adapt to evolving threats and changing business needs.

1.7 SOFTWARE DEVELOPMENT LIFE CYCLE

The Software Development Life Cycle (SDLC) is a structured process that outlines the various stages involved in developing software, from initial planning to deployment and maintenance. Understanding the SDLC is crucial for integrating security considerations throughout the entire development process. Traditional SDLC models, such as Waterfall and Agile, provide a framework for managing software projects but often lack sufficient emphasis on security.

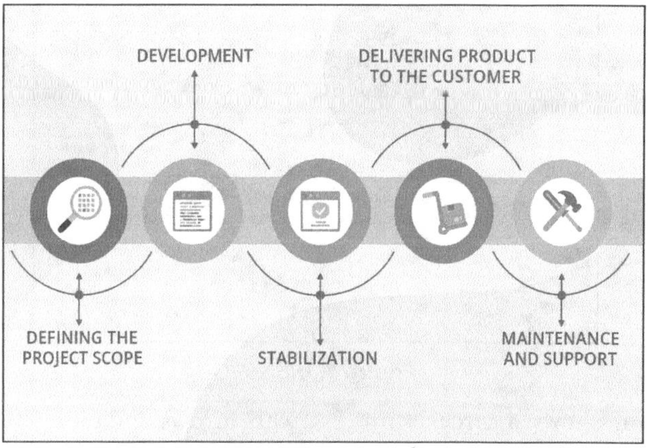

***Figure 1.2:** Software Development Life Cycle*

Figure 1.2 illustrates a simplified software or project development lifecycle, represented as a series of connected steps within a timeline:

- **Defining the Project Scope:** This initial stage, depicted with a magnifying glass inspecting a grid, emphasizes the importance of clearly defining the project's goals, objectives, and boundaries.
- **Development:** Represented with code on a screen, this stage involves the actual coding, building, and creating the software or project.
- **Stabilization:** Shown with a checkmark icon, this indicates the phase where the product is tested, refined, and made stable for release.
- **Delivering Product to the Customer:** A cart with a box symbolizes the product being delivered to the end-user.
- **Maintenance and Support:** With a hammer and wrench icon, this final stage represents the ongoing support, updates, and maintenance required to keep the product running smoothly.

Recognizing the importance of security, the Secure SDLC (SSDLC) integrates security activities into each phase of the development process. This involves incorporating security requirements early in the planning phase, conducting threat modeling and security risk assessments during the design phase, performing code reviews and security testing during the implementation phase, and implementing security monitoring and incident response procedures during the maintenance phase. Shifting security "left" in the SDLC is key.

By integrating security activities into each phase of the SDLC, organizations can identify and address security vulnerabilities early, reducing the cost and effort required to remediate them later. This approach ensures that security is not an afterthought but a fundamental consideration throughout the software development lifecycle. A well-defined and implemented SSDLC helps create more secure and reliable software products.

1.8 SECURITY SYSTEMS DEVELOPMENT LIFE CYCLE

The Security Systems Development Life Cycle (SSDLC) is a structured framework for developing and implementing secure systems. It builds upon the traditional SDLC by incorporating security considerations at every stage. The SSDLC phases are as given in figure 1.3.

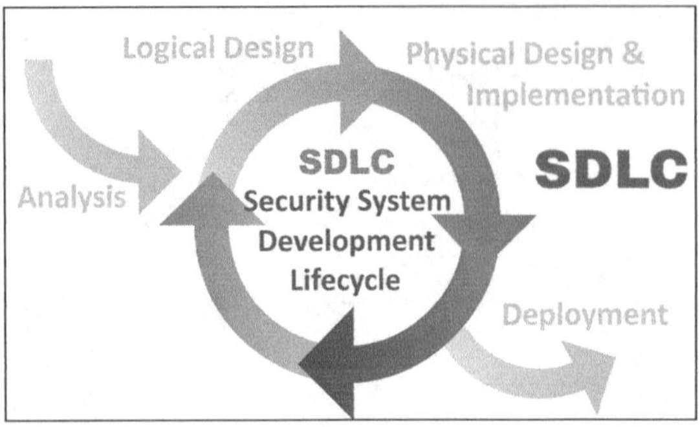

Figure 1.3: *SSDLC*

The diagram shows a circular process with arrows indicating the flow between different stages. The central label indicates that the process represents the "Security System Development Lifecycle." The main stages represented are as follows:

- **Analysis**: This stage involves assessing the current security posture, identifying vulnerabilities, and determining security requirements. The goal is to understand the organization's security needs and the potential risks.
- **Logical Design**: In this stage, a security architecture is designed based on the findings from the analysis stage. This includes selecting appropriate security controls, defining security policies, and designing the overall structure of the security system.
- **Physical Design & Implementation**: This stage involves the actual implementation of the security controls and architecture designed in the previous stage. This includes configuring security devices, implementing security software, and integrating security measures into existing systems.
- **Deployment**: This stage is where the implemented security system is put into operation. It includes deploying security controls, training users on security procedures, and ensuring the system is functioning as intended.

The continuous, cyclical nature of the diagram emphasizes that the SSDLC is an ongoing process. After deployment, the system needs to be continuously monitored, maintained, and updated to address new threats and vulnerabilities. The arrows show that after deployment, the process should loop back to the analysis stage to reassess the security needs and adapt the system accordingly.

1.9 SECURITY PROFESSIONALS AND THE ORGANIZATION

Security professionals play a crucial role in safeguarding an organization's digital assets, and their expertise and dedication are essential for maintaining a strong security posture. Different security roles exist within an organization, each with specific responsibilities and skill sets. These roles may include security analysts, security architects, incident responders, and Chief Information Security Officers (CISOs).

Building a dedicated security team is vital for effectively managing and mitigating security risks. The security team is responsible for implementing security controls, monitoring for security incidents, and responding to breaches. The CISO, as the leader of the security team, plays a strategic role in aligning security efforts with the organization's overall business objectives.

Creating a security-aware culture within the organization is equally important. Security professionals need to communicate security risks and best practices to employees across all departments. Regular training and awareness programs can empower employees to recognize and avoid potential threats, contributing to a stronger overall security posture. The organization's overall culture must emphasize security at all levels.

Video Resources

- **Cybersecurity Basics:** https://www.youtube.com/watch?v=iNC6iPYHQtQ
- **CIA Triad Explained:** https://www.youtube.com/watch?v=4IlHg409eSQ
- **Non-Repudiation, Authentication and Authorization:** https://www.youtube.com/watch?v=z1vC9Jm28E
- **What is Malware?** https://www.youtube.com/watch?v=qmK06Z0wE-I
- **Phishing Explained :** https://www.youtube.com/watch?v=sb39Rq2X-Es
- **Firewalls Explained :** https://www.youtube.com/watch?v=fqiEvGwtV5I
- **The Importance of Cybersecurity:** https://www.youtube.com/watch?v=bWmSvehXA8U

Use of ICT

The effective use of ICT is crucial across all aspects of cybersecurity, from implementing preventive measures like Role-Based Access Control (RBAC) and Multi-Factor Authentication (MFA) for secure access management, to employing encryption techniques such as AES (Advanced Encryption Standard) and TLS (Transport Layer Security) for protecting data at rest and in transit. Network security relies heavily on ICT through firewalls for controlling traffic and Intrusion Prevention Systems (IPS) for detecting and preventing vulnerability exploits.

Detection and monitoring benefit from ICT through Intrusion Detection Systems (IDS) utilizing signature-based and anomaly-based detection and Security Information and Event Management (SIEM) for real-time analysis of security alerts, while incident response and recovery leverage ICT for data backup, restoration, and post-incident analysis. Ethical hacking, threat modeling, vulnerability assessments, security training programs and security policies also rely on ICT as they develop the cybersecurity landscape within an organization.

SUMMARY

Introduction to Cybersecurity

- Cybersecurity protects computer systems, networks, and data from digital attacks, unauthorized access, and damage.
- It is crucial due to the increasing reliance on internet-connected devices and the digitization of personal and professional lives.
- Core concepts include confidentiality, integrity, and availability.
- Authentication, authorization, and non-repudiation are also key components.
- Effective cybersecurity requires constant vigilance and a proactive approach.

Need for Security

- Protecting personal information prevents identity theft, fraud, and personal harm.
- Securing corporate data maintains competitive advantage, customer trust, and legal compliance.
- Safeguarding government information protects national security.
- Cybersecurity prevents financial loss from attacks like ransomware and phishing.
- It supports economic stability by ensuring the integrity of financial systems.
- Cybersecurity ensures operational continuity by preventing disruptions to business operations.
- Legal and regulatory compliance requires robust cybersecurity measures.
- Protecting intellectual property prevents theft and espionage.
- Safeguarding privacy protects individuals in their digital interactions.

Security Approaches

- Preventive measures include access control (RBAC, MFA), encryption (AES, TLS, PKI), and network security (firewalls, IPS).
- Detection and monitoring use intrusion detection systems (IDS) with signature-based and anomaly-based detection.
- Security Information and Event Management (SIEM) provides log management and real-time monitoring.
- Response and mitigation involve incident response plans (IRP) and teams.
- Disaster recovery plans (DRP) and business continuity plans (BCP) ensure essential functions continue during disasters.
- Mitigation and risk management include risk assessment with threat modeling and vulnerability assessment.
- Penetration testing uses ethical hacking and Red/Blue Team exercises.
- Recovery involves data backup and restoration with secure storage.
- Post-incident analysis includes root cause analysis and lessons learned.
- Awareness and training include employee training and security policies.

Principles of Security

- Confidentiality ensures sensitive information is accessible only to authorized individuals through encryption and access controls.
- Integrity maintains data accuracy throughout its lifecycle, using hash functions and digital signatures.
- Availability ensures resources are accessible when needed through redundancy and disaster recovery planning.
- Non-repudiation ensures parties cannot deny actions using digital signatures and audit logs.
- Authentication verifies user identities with passwords, biometrics, and multi-factor authentication.
- Authorization determines what actions authenticated users can perform via role-based access control (RBAC).

EXERCISES

A. Subjective Questions

Category-I (Revised Bloom's Level - 1, 2 & 3): Knowledge, Comprehension, Application

1. Define cybersecurity and explain its importance in today's digital world. (Level 1, Knowledge)
2. Describe the core concepts of cybersecurity: confidentiality, integrity, and availability. Provide a real-world example for each concept. (Level 2, Comprehension)
3. Explain how a firewall works to protect a network. (Level 2, Comprehension)
4. What are the steps an organization should take to respond to a confirmed cybersecurity incident? (Level 3, Application)
5. Explain the difference between authentication and authorization. (Level 2 Comprehension)
6. Describe a situation when multi factor authentication should be required. (Level 3 Application)

Category-II (Revised Bloom's Level - 4, 5 & 6): Analysis, Synthesis, Evaluation

1. Analyze the trade-offs between implementing strict security measures and maintaining user accessibility. How can an organization effectively balance these competing priorities? (Level 4, Analysis)
2. Design a security awareness training program for employees that addresses phishing attacks and password security. (Level 6, Create)
3. Evaluate the effectiveness of different authentication methods (passwords, biometrics, multi-factor authentication) in various scenarios. What are the strengths and weaknesses of each? (Level 5, Evaluate)
4. Discuss the ethical implications of using data masking and tokenization techniques to protect sensitive data. (Level 6, Evaluate)
5. Given a scenario of a security breach, analyze the existing security approaches and design an improved solution to avoid further breaches. (Level 6 Create)

B. Objective Questions

Category-I (Revised Bloom's Level - 1, 2 & 3): Knowledge, Comprehension, Application

1. Which of the following is NOT a core concept of cybersecurity? (Level 1, Knowledge)
   (a) Confidentiality (b) Integrity
   (c) Availability (d) Usability
2. Which type of cyber threat involves disguising as a trustworthy entity to obtain sensitive information? (Level 1, Knowledge)
   (a) Malware (b) Phishing
   (c) DoS (d) SQL Injection

3. What is the purpose of encryption? (Level 2, Comprehension)
   (a) To prevent unauthorized access to a network
   (b) To convert information into a secure format
   (c) To detect malicious activity
   (d) To manage security alerts
4. Which security measure involves monitoring network traffic for malicious activity or policy violations? (Level 2, Comprehension)
   (a) Firewall (b) Antivirus Software
   (c) Intrusion Detection System (d) Encryption

Category-II (Revised Bloom's Level - 4, 5 & 6): Analysis, Synthesis, Evaluation

1. Which of the following security approaches would be most effective in preventing a zero-day exploit? (Level 5, Evaluation)
   (a) Signature-based IDS (b) Anomaly-based IDS
   (c) Antivirus software (d) Firewall
2. Which security principle is most directly violated by a denial-of-service (DoS) attack? (Level 4, Analysis)
   (a) Confidentiality (b) Integrity
   (c) Availability (d) Non-repudiation
3. Which of the following methods would BEST ensure data integrity? (Level 5, Evaluation)
   (a) Encryption (b) Access Controls
   (c) Data Masking (d) Hashing Algorithms
4. An organisation wants to ensure that it can continue essential business function after a cyber security attack. which approach is best to follow (Level 5, Application)
   (a) Incident Response Plan (b) Business Continuity Plan
   (c) Vulnerability assesment (d) Patch management

TEACHER'S KNOW MORE

For teachers seeking to enrich their instruction on Unit 1: Introduction to Cybersecurity, it's beneficial to emphasize real-world examples of security breaches and their impacts to illustrate the practical implications of the concepts discussed, encourage students to explore current cybersecurity news and events to foster critical thinking and awareness, and facilitate discussions on the ethical considerations surrounding cybersecurity, such as privacy, data security, and responsible use of technology. Furthermore, incorporating hands-on activities, like setting up a basic firewall or practicing password management, can provide students with valuable practical skills, while also highlighting the importance of a holistic approach to security that combines technical measures with user awareness and organizational policies, thus preparing them to be informed and responsible digital citizens and future cybersecurity professionals.

2 UNIT Cybersecurity – Threats & Attacks

RATIONALE

This chapter, "Cybersecurity Threats and Attacks," is crucial for building a practical understanding of the risks facing modern digital environments. While theoretical knowledge of security principles is essential, it's equally important to understand the real-world threats that those principles are designed to defend against. The chapter provides a detailed overview of various threats, including intellectual property theft, software attacks, and human error, highlighting the diverse nature of potential security breaches and how they impact systems.The rationale continues with an examination of a wide array of attack methods, from malicious code and denial-of-service attacks to social engineering and pharming. This section is vital for giving students actionable information and a comprehensive understanding of attack vectors. By understanding how these attacks work, security professionals can better anticipate and defend against them. The broad survey ensures that readers gain a solid foundation in the current threat landscape.Finally, this knowledge base enables security professionals to develop targeted security measures, conduct effective risk assessments, and implement appropriate incident response plans. In conclusion, a deep understanding of these threats and attacks is foundational for anyone involved in protecting digital assets and is a fundamental cornerstone in any cybersecurity curriculum.

UNIT OUTCOMES

- **Understand the diversity of cybersecurity threats**, including intellectual property theft, software attacks, and espionage, recognizing the varying motivations and impacts of these threats on organizations.
- **Identify common attack vectors**, such as malicious code, social engineering, and DoS/DDoS attacks, gaining insight into how attackers exploit vulnerabilities to compromise systems and networks.
- **Analyze the role of human factors in security breaches**, assessing how human error, missing policies, and inadequate controls can contribute to successful attacks and data compromise.
- **Evaluate the impact of environmental factors and disruptions**, considering how forces of nature, hardware failures, and software failures can lead to data loss, system downtime, and business interruption.
- **Develop mitigation strategies for various threats and attacks**, including implementing robust security controls, enhancing user awareness, and establishing effective incident response plans to minimize risk and ensure business continuity.

2.1 THREATS: INTELLECTUAL PROPERTY

Intellectual property (IP) refers to creations of the mind, such as inventions, literary and artistic works, designs, and symbols, names, and images used in commerce. The theft of intellectual property is a significant threat in the digital age, often motivated by financial gain or competitive advantage. This type of theft can involve stealing trade secrets, patented inventions, copyrighted materials, or proprietary data. The consequences can be devastating for businesses, leading to loss of revenue, market share, and competitive edge.

Cybercriminals employ various methods to steal intellectual property, including hacking into corporate networks, phishing employees for credentials, and using malware to exfiltrate sensitive data. Insider threats also pose a significant risk, as disgruntled employees or contractors may intentionally leak or steal valuable information. The value of intellectual property makes it a high-priority target for both internal and external threat actors, necessitating robust security measures.

Protecting intellectual property requires a multi-layered approach. This includes implementing strong access controls, encrypting sensitive data, monitoring network traffic for suspicious activity, and conducting regular security audits. Employee training is also crucial to raise awareness about the risks of IP theft and how to recognize and report potential threats. Furthermore, legal measures such as non-disclosure agreements (NDAs) and intellectual property rights enforcement are essential components of a comprehensive IP protection strategy.

Effective intellectual property protection requires continuous monitoring and adaptation to the evolving threat landscape. Staying informed about the latest cyber threats and implementing proactive security measures are essential for safeguarding valuable intellectual assets. Organizations must also foster a culture of security awareness and prioritize intellectual property protection at all levels to mitigate the risk of theft and maintain a competitive advantage.

2.2 SOFTWARE ATTACKS

Software attacks exploit vulnerabilities in software applications and operating systems to compromise systems, steal data, or disrupt operations. These attacks can range from simple exploits of known vulnerabilities to sophisticated, zero-day attacks that target previously unknown flaws. Common software attacks include buffer overflows, SQL injection, cross-site scripting (XSS), and remote code execution vulnerabilities. The impact of software attacks can be severe, leading to data breaches, system downtime, and financial losses.

Buffer overflow attacks occur when a program writes data beyond the allocated buffer, potentially overwriting adjacent memory locations and executing malicious code. SQL injection attacks involve inserting malicious SQL queries into input fields, allowing attackers to bypass authentication and gain unauthorized access to databases. Cross-site scripting (XSS) attacks inject malicious scripts into trusted websites, allowing attackers to steal user credentials or redirect users to malicious sites.

Preventing software attacks requires a proactive approach that includes secure coding practices, regular software updates, and vulnerability scanning. Developers should adhere to secure coding guidelines to minimize the risk of introducing vulnerabilities into their code. Organizations should also implement a robust patch management process to promptly apply security updates and address known vulnerabilities. Web application firewalls (WAFs) can help protect against common web-based attacks like SQL injection and XSS.

Regular penetration testing and vulnerability assessments are essential for identifying and addressing potential weaknesses in software applications. These tests simulate real-world attacks to uncover vulnerabilities and assess the effectiveness of existing security controls. By staying vigilant and implementing proactive security measures, organizations can significantly reduce their risk of falling victim to software attacks and protect their critical systems and data.

2.3 DEVIATIONS IN QOS

Deviations in Quality of Service (QoS) refer to disruptions or degradations in the performance of network services, affecting the user experience and potentially indicating malicious activity. These deviations can manifest as increased latency, packet loss, jitter, or reduced bandwidth, leading to slow response times, dropped connections, and overall poor performance. Deviations in QoS can be caused by various factors, including network congestion, hardware failures, software bugs, or malicious attacks.

Denial-of-service (DoS) and distributed denial-of-service (DDoS) attacks are common causes of QoS deviations. These attacks flood network resources with traffic, overwhelming servers and network infrastructure, making them unavailable to legitimate users. Malware infections, misconfigured network devices, and faulty software can also lead to QoS issues, disrupting network services and impacting business operations.

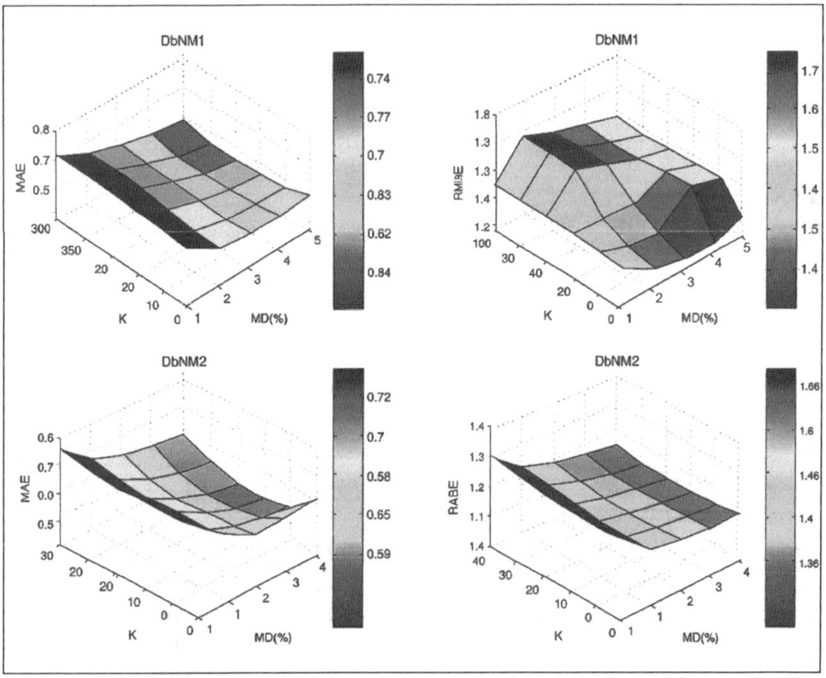

Figure 2.1: *Performance of deviation based neighborhood models with different k and matrix density*

There are four plots in total, arranged in a 2×2 grid. This suggests we're comparing different models or different performance metrics for the same models. Each plot is a 3D surface plot. This is used to visualize how a dependent variable (performance metric) changes as a function of two independent variables.

- **X-axis (labeled 'K'):** This most likely represents the number of neighbors used in the neighborhood model. The values range from 0 to 320. "K" represents the "k" in k-nearest neighbors.
- **Y-axis (labeled 'MD(%)'):** This likely stands for "Matrix Density (%)," which refers to the percentage of available data. This represents the number of known entries in relation to missing entries. The values range from 0 to 5.

- **Z-axis (vertical axis):** There are two different metrics of performance presented, that are MAE and RMSE.
  - **MAE - Mean Absolute Error:** In the two plots on the left hand side the vertical axis represents MAE.
  - **RMSE - Root Mean Square Error:** In the two plots on the right hand side the vertical axis represents RMSE.

Plots

- DbNM1 MAE (Top left):
  - Represents the mean absolute error for DbNM1 model.
- DbNM1 RMSE (Top Right):
  - Represents the root mean square error for DbNM1 model.
- DbNM2 MAE (Bottom left):
  - Represents the mean absolute error for DbNM2 model.
- DbNM2 RMSE (Bottom Right):
  - Represents the root mean square error for DbNM2 model.

How to Interpret

- **Lower is Better:** In general, for both MAE and RMSE, lower values indicate better performance. A model with lower error is more accurate in its predictions.
- **Trends:** Look for trends in the surfaces. As K (number of neighbors) or MD (matrix density) increases, how does the MAE or RMSE change? Is there a clear improvement or degradation in performance? Are there regions where the model performs particularly well or poorly?
- **Comparison:** Compare the surfaces between DbNM1 and DbNM2. Which model seems to have lower overall error? How does the performance of the two models differ as a function of K and MD?

The figure 2.1 presents a performance analysis of two deviation-based neighborhood models (DbNM1 and DbNM2) for QoS deviation prediction. The plots show how the MAE and RMSE change as a function of the number of neighbors (K) and the matrix density (MD). By comparing the surfaces, you can determine which model performs better under different conditions. Remember that lower values on the z-axis (MAE and RMSE) indicate better prediction accuracy.

Monitoring network performance and establishing baseline QoS metrics are essential for detecting deviations. Network monitoring tools can track key performance indicators (KPIs) such as latency, packet loss, and bandwidth utilization, alerting administrators to any significant deviations from established baselines. Analyzing network traffic patterns and identifying anomalies can help pinpoint the root cause of QoS issues.

Addressing deviations in QoS requires a multi-faceted approach that includes network optimization, traffic shaping, and implementing security controls to mitigate malicious attacks. Load balancing can distribute traffic across multiple servers to prevent overload, while traffic shaping techniques prioritize critical applications and limit bandwidth consumption by non-essential services. Intrusion detection and prevention systems (IDS/IPS) can help identify and block malicious traffic associated with DoS and DDoS attacks, restoring normal QoS levels.

2.4 ESPIONAGE, FORCES OF NATURE, HUMAN ERROR, INFORMATION EXTORTION

Espionage, whether state-sponsored or corporate, poses a significant threat to sensitive information and national security. Cyber espionage involves the use of cyberattacks to steal classified information, trade secrets, or intellectual property. These attacks are often highly targeted and sophisticated, employing advanced techniques to bypass security controls and exfiltrate data without detection. The consequences of successful espionage can include loss of competitive advantage, damage to national security, and compromised diplomatic relations.

Figure 2.2: *Cyber Espionage*

Espionage, at its core, is the practice of obtaining information that is considered secret or confidential without the permission of the holder of the information. It's often associated with national security, but it can also occur in corporate settings, particularly to gain a competitive advantage. Espionage can take many forms, depending on the goals, resources, and risks involved.

Here are some common types of espionage.

- **Human Intelligence (HUMINT):** This is the oldest form of espionage, relying on human spies to gather information through interpersonal contact. It involves cultivating sources, building relationships, and extracting information discreetly. HUMINT can be risky, as it relies on trust and can be compromised if a source is unreliable or exposed.
- **Signals Intelligence (SIGINT):** This involves intercepting and analyzing electronic signals, such as communications between individuals, radar signals, or other forms of electronic transmission. SIGINT is often used to gather information about military activities, diplomatic communications, or other strategic interests.
- **Cyber Espionage:** This involves using computer networks and systems to gain unauthorized access to sensitive information. It can involve hacking into computer systems, stealing data, or planting malware to monitor activity. Cyber espionage is becoming increasingly common as more information is stored and transmitted electronically.
- **Open-Source Intelligence (OSINT):** This involves collecting and analyzing information from publicly available sources, such as news articles, social media, academic publications, and government reports. While OSINT doesn't involve clandestine activities, it can be a valuable source of information for intelligence agencies and businesses.
- **Imagery Intelligence (IMINT):** This involves collecting and analyzing images, such as satellite photos, aerial photographs, and other forms of visual data. IMINT can be used to monitor military activities, track environmental changes, or assess infrastructure damage.

- **Financial Espionage:** This type of espionage is focused on obtaining information about financial institutions, markets, or transactions. It can involve stealing trade secrets, insider trading, or other forms of financial crime.
- **Industrial Espionage:** Also known as corporate espionage, focuses on stealing proprietary information from competitors for commercial gain. This can include trade secrets, patents, customer lists, or marketing strategies.

It's important to note that espionage is often illegal and can have serious consequences, depending on the laws of the countries involved. However, it remains a persistent activity in both the political and corporate worlds.

Forces of nature, such as earthquakes, floods, hurricanes, and wildfires, can cause significant disruptions to IT infrastructure and data centers. These events can lead to hardware damage, power outages, and network disruptions, resulting in data loss, system downtime, and business interruption. Preparing for natural disasters requires robust disaster recovery plans, including offsite backups, redundant systems, and emergency power sources.

Human error as given in figure 2.3 is a common cause of security incidents and data breaches. Mistakes made by employees, such as misconfiguring systems, falling victim to phishing attacks, or mishandling sensitive data, can create vulnerabilities that attackers can exploit. Implementing strong security awareness training programs and enforcing strict security policies are essential for minimizing the risk of human error.

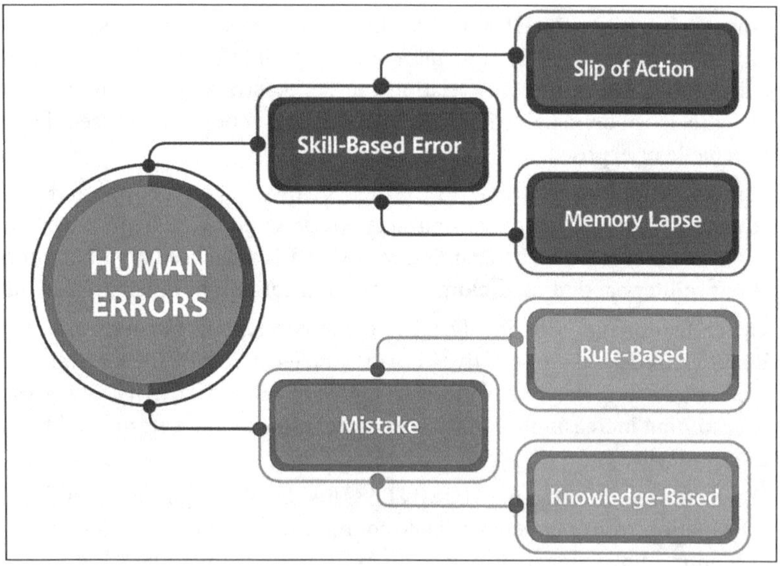

Figure 2.3: *Human error*

Information extortion as given in figure 2.4 involves the use of threats or coercion to obtain sensitive information or financial gain. Ransomware attacks, where attackers encrypt data and demand a ransom for its release, are a common form of information extortion. Other tactics include threatening to release sensitive data publicly or to competitors unless a ransom is paid. Preventing information extortion requires robust security controls, including strong backups, incident response plans, and employee training to recognize and avoid extortion attempts.

Figure 2.4: *Information Extortion*

2.5 MISSING, INADEQUATE, OR INCOMPLETE ORGANIZATION POLICY

Missing, inadequate, or incomplete organizational policies create significant vulnerabilities that cybercriminals can exploit. Without clear and comprehensive policies, employees may lack guidance on acceptable behavior, data handling procedures, and security protocols, leading to inconsistent security practices and increased risk. A strong policy framework is essential for establishing a security culture and providing a foundation for effective security controls.

Common policy deficiencies include a lack of clear guidelines on password management, data access controls, remote access security, and incident response procedures. Without explicit policies, employees may use weak passwords, share credentials, store sensitive data insecurely, or fail to report security incidents promptly. These gaps in policy can create opportunities for attackers to gain unauthorized access to systems and data.

Developing comprehensive security policies requires a thorough understanding of the organization's business operations, risk profile, and legal and regulatory requirements. Policies should be clear, concise, and easily accessible to all employees. Regular review and updates are essential to ensure that policies remain relevant and effective in addressing emerging threats.

Effective policy enforcement is crucial for ensuring compliance and maintaining a strong security posture. Organizations should implement mechanisms for monitoring adherence to policies and providing training and awareness programs to educate employees about their responsibilities. Consistent enforcement of policies, coupled with ongoing communication and feedback, can help foster a culture of security awareness and accountability.

2.6 MISSING, INADEQUATE, OR INCOMPLETE CONTROLS

Missing, inadequate, or incomplete security controls leave organizations vulnerable to a wide range of cyber threats. Security controls are the safeguards and countermeasures implemented to protect systems, networks, and data from unauthorized access, use, disclosure, disruption, modification, or destruction. Without adequate controls, organizations may be unable to prevent, detect, or respond to security incidents effectively.

Common control deficiencies include a lack of strong authentication mechanisms, inadequate access controls, insufficient monitoring and logging, and missing data encryption. Weak passwords, shared credentials, and unrestricted access to sensitive data create opportunities for attackers to compromise systems and steal information. Insufficient logging and monitoring make it difficult to detect and investigate security incidents, while missing data encryption leaves sensitive data vulnerable to unauthorized disclosure.

Implementing effective security controls requires a risk-based approach that prioritizes controls based on the potential impact and likelihood of threats. Organizations should conduct regular risk assessments to identify vulnerabilities and determine the appropriate level of security controls needed to mitigate those risks. A defense-in-depth strategy, which involves implementing multiple layers of security controls, can provide enhanced protection against a variety of attacks.

Regular testing and validation of security controls are essential for ensuring their effectiveness. Penetration testing, vulnerability assessments, and security audits can help identify weaknesses in existing controls and provide recommendations for improvement. By continuously monitoring, testing, and improving security controls, organizations can maintain a strong security posture and protect their critical assets.

2.7 SABOTAGE, THEFT, HARDWARE FAILURES

Sabotage involves intentional acts of destruction or disruption aimed at harming an organization's systems, data, or operations. Sabotage can be carried out by disgruntled employees, competitors, or malicious actors seeking to cause damage or disrupt business activities. The consequences of sabotage can be severe, including data loss, system downtime, reputational damage, and financial losses.

Theft of hardware, such as laptops, servers, and storage devices, can result in data breaches and loss of critical assets. Stolen devices may contain sensitive information that can be exploited by attackers, leading to identity theft, financial fraud, or disclosure of confidential business data. Implementing strong physical security measures, such as access controls, surveillance systems, and asset tracking, can help prevent hardware theft.

Hardware failures, such as hard drive crashes, server malfunctions, and network outages, can cause data loss, system downtime, and business interruption. While hardware failures are often unintentional, they can have a significant impact on an organization's operations. Implementing redundancy, backups, and disaster recovery plans can help mitigate the impact of hardware failures and ensure business continuity.

Preventing sabotage, theft, and hardware failures requires a combination of physical security measures, technical controls, and proactive maintenance. Employee background checks, access controls, and surveillance systems can help deter sabotage and theft. Implementing redundant systems, regular backups, and disaster recovery plans can help minimize the impact of hardware failures and ensure business continuity.

2.8 SOFTWARE FAILURES ATTACKS: MALICIOUS CODE

Malicious code refers to software designed to infiltrate computer systems, damage or disrupt operations, steal data, or gain unauthorized access. This includes viruses, worms, Trojan horses, ransomware, spyware, and other types of malware. Malicious code can be delivered through various means, including email attachments, malicious websites, infected USB drives, and software vulnerabilities. The impact of malicious code attacks can range from minor inconveniences to catastrophic data breaches and system outages.

Viruses are malicious programs that attach themselves to executable files and spread to other systems when infected files are executed. Worms are self-replicating programs that spread across networks without requiring human interaction. Trojan horses are malicious programs disguised as legitimate software, tricking users into installing them. Ransomware encrypts data and demands a ransom for its release, while spyware collects information about users without their knowledge or consent.

Preventing malicious code attacks requires a multi-layered approach that includes antivirus software, firewalls, intrusion detection systems, and user education. Antivirus software can detect and remove known malware, while firewalls can block malicious traffic from entering the network. Intrusion detection systems can identify suspicious activity and alert administrators to potential infections.

Employee training is crucial for raising awareness about the risks of malicious code and how to recognize and avoid potential threats. Users should be educated about the dangers of clicking on suspicious links, opening untrusted attachments, and downloading software from untrusted sources. Regular software updates and patch management are essential for addressing known vulnerabilities that can be exploited by malicious code.

2.9 HOAXES, BACK DOORS, PASSWORD CRACKS, BRUTE FORCE, DICTIONARY

Hoaxes are deceptive messages or warnings designed to trick users into performing actions that can compromise their security or disrupt their operations. Hoaxes often spread through email, social media, or other communication channels, preying on users' fears or curiosity. While hoaxes may not directly install malicious code, they can cause confusion, waste time, and lead users to take actions that make them vulnerable to real threats.

Back doors are hidden entry points into a system that allow attackers to bypass normal security controls and gain unauthorized access. Back doors can be intentionally created by developers for debugging purposes or unintentionally introduced through coding errors. Attackers can exploit back doors to install malware, steal data, or disrupt system operations.

Password cracking techniques are used to recover passwords from stored data or transmitted data. Brute-force attacks involve trying every possible combination of characters until the correct password is found. Dictionary attacks use lists of common words and phrases to guess passwords. Password cracking attacks can be used to gain unauthorized access to systems, accounts, and sensitive data.

Preventing hoaxes, back doors, and password cracking requires a combination of technical controls, security policies, and user education. Strong password policies, multi-factor authentication, and regular password audits can help prevent password cracking attacks. Code reviews and security testing can help identify and remove back doors from software applications. Employee training can raise awareness about the risks of hoaxes and how to avoid falling victim to deceptive messages.

2.10 DOS AND DDOS, SPOOFING, MAN-IN-THE-MIDDLE, SPAM

Denial-of-Service (DoS) and Distributed Denial-of-Service (DDoS) attacks overwhelm a system or network with traffic, making it unavailable to legitimate users. DoS attacks originate from a single source, while DDoS attacks come from multiple sources, making them more difficult to defend against. DoS and DDoS attacks can disrupt websites, online services, and critical infrastructure, causing significant financial losses and reputational damage.

The figure 2.5 illustrates the fundamental difference between a Denial of Service (DoS) attack and a Distributed Denial of Service (DDoS) attack. The key distinction lies in the source and scale of the attack.

Denial of Service (DoS) Attack

- **Single System Source:** A DoS attack originates from a single computer or network connection. In the diagram, a single computer is shown sending traffic towards a server.
- **Overwhelms Resources:** The goal of a DoS attack is to overwhelm the target system (e.g., a server, application, or network) with traffic, requests, or malicious code, rendering it unable to respond to legitimate users. This leads to service disruption or complete unavailability.

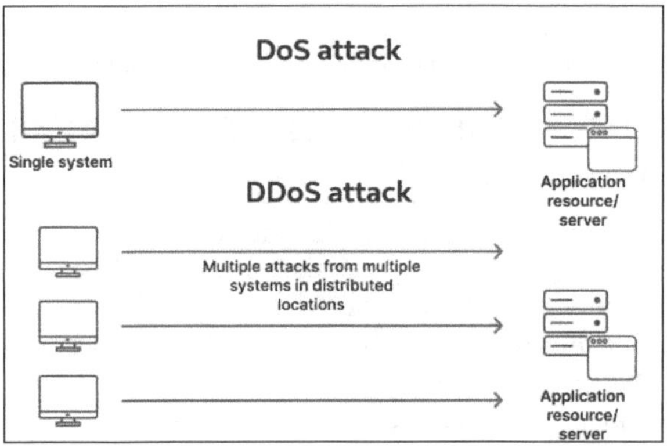

Figure 2.5: DoS & DDoS attacks

Distributed Denial of Service (DDoS) Attack

- **Multiple, Distributed Sources:** A DDoS attack originates from numerous computers or devices, often spread across different locations. The diagram depicts multiple computers, each sending traffic to the same target server.
- **Botnet or Compromised Systems:** DDoS attacks typically utilize a botnet, which is a network of compromised computers (often infected with malware) that are controlled by an attacker. The attacker can then command the botnet to flood the target system with malicious traffic.
- **Increased Scale and Impact:** Due to the distributed nature and scale of DDoS attacks, they are often more difficult to mitigate than DoS attacks. The sheer volume of traffic can overwhelm even well-protected systems.

In essence, the diagram highlights that a DoS attack is like a single person blocking a doorway, while a DDoS attack is like a mob overwhelming the same doorway from many directions.

Spoofing involves disguising communication to appear as if it originates from a trusted source. Spoofing can be used in various attacks, including email spoofing, IP address spoofing, and DNS spoofing. Email spoofing involves forging the sender's address to trick recipients into opening malicious attachments or clicking on phishing links. IP address spoofing involves using a false IP address to hide the origin of an attack or bypass security controls. Figure 2.6 shows how IP Spoofing works.

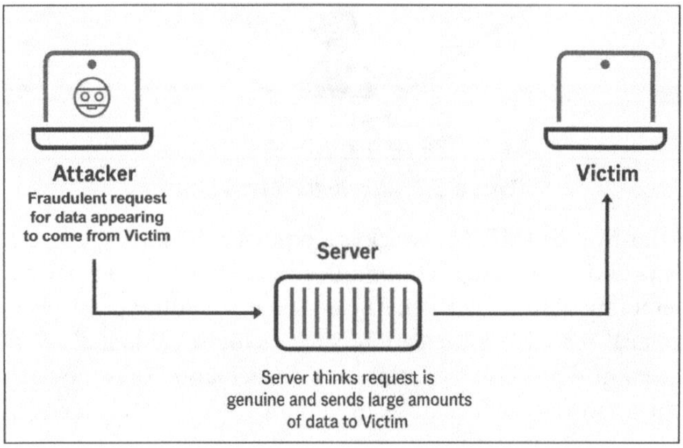

Figure 2.6: *How IP Spoofing Works*

Spoofing is a cybersecurity tactic where attackers disguise themselves as trusted entities to deceive victims and gain access to sensitive information, systems, or assets. This deceptive practice can take various forms, including email spoofing, where the sender's address is forged to appear legitimate; caller ID spoofing, which manipulates phone numbers; and website or URL spoofing, where fake websites mimic trusted ones to harvest credentials. Spoofing often relies on social engineering techniques to exploit human vulnerabilities like trust and urgency, making it a potent tool for spreading malware, stealing data, or committing fraud.

Attackers use spoofing to bypass security defenses by impersonating known sources. For example, in DNS spoofing (or cache poisoning), hackers redirect traffic from legitimate websites to malicious ones by exploiting vulnerabilities in the Domain Name System. Similarly, IP spoofing involves forging the source IP address in data packets to impersonate another system. These attacks can lead to severe consequences such as unauthorized access, data breaches, or financial losses. Spoofing also plays a role in broader cyberattacks like man-in-the-middle (MITM) attacks, where attackers intercept and manipulate communications between two parties.

To protect against spoofing, individuals and organizations should adopt robust cybersecurity measures. These include using multi-factor authentication (MFA), verifying the legitimacy of communication sources, and employing advanced email security tools to detect and block spoofed messages. Additionally, ensuring websites use HTTPS and educating users about identifying phishing attempts can mitigate risks. Regularly updating software and implementing network monitoring solutions further enhance defenses against this pervasive threat.

Man-in-the-Middle (MitM) attacks as given in figure 2.7 intercepts communication between two parties without their knowledge, allowing attackers to eavesdrop, steal data, or modify messages. MitM attacks can be carried out by intercepting network traffic, compromising DNS servers, or using rogue Wi-Fi hotspots. MitM attacks can be used to steal login credentials, credit card numbers, and other sensitive information.

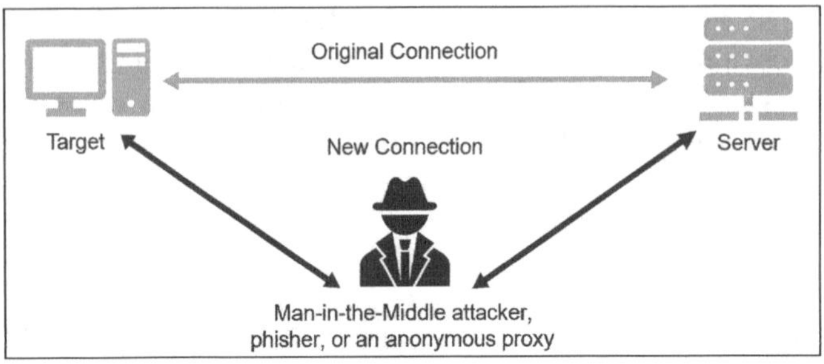

***Figure 2.7:** Man in the Middle Attack*

A Man-in-the-Middle (MITM) attack is a type of cyberattack where a malicious actor secretly intercepts and manipulates communication between two parties who believe they are directly interacting with each other. The attacker can either passively eavesdrop on the conversation to steal sensitive information, such as login credentials or financial data, or actively alter the communication to mislead the participants. These attacks typically exploit vulnerabilities in networks, such as unsecured public Wi-Fi or weak encryption protocols, making them a significant threat to online security.

MITM attacks generally involve two stages: interception and decryption. In the interception phase, attackers position themselves between the victim and their intended recipient by creating fake Wi-Fi hotspots or breaching network devices. Once in place, they gain access to all data exchanged. In the decryption phase, attackers may use techniques like SSL stripping to downgrade secure HTTPS connections to less secure HTTP ones, enabling them to read encrypted data. Common forms of MITM attacks include session hijacking, replay attacks, and phishing schemes that trick users into divulging sensitive information.

To defend against MITM attacks, users should adopt robust cybersecurity practices. This includes avoiding public Wi-Fi for sensitive transactions, using Virtual Private Networks (VPNs) for encrypted communication, and ensuring websites use HTTPS connections. Multi-factor authentication and regularly updating software also add layers of protection. Organizations can implement advanced security protocols like end-to-end encryption and intrusion detection systems to mitigate risks further. Awareness and vigilance remain key in identifying potential threats and securing personal and professional communications from MITM attacks.

Spam refers to unsolicited and unwanted messages, typically sent in bulk via email or other electronic communication channels. Spam can be used to deliver malware, phishing attacks, or fraudulent offers. Spam filters can help block unwanted messages, but attackers are constantly developing new techniques to bypass these filters.

Preventing DoS/DDoS attacks, spoofing, MitM attacks, and spam requires a multi-layered approach that includes network security controls, authentication mechanisms, encryption, and user education. Firewalls, intrusion detection systems, and content filters can help block malicious traffic and spam. Strong authentication protocols, such as multi-factor authentication, can help prevent spoofing and MitM attacks.

2.11 EMAIL BOMBING, SNIFFERS

Email bombing is a type of denial-of-service (DoS) attack that overwhelms a victim's email inbox with a massive volume of messages, rendering it unusable. Attackers use automated tools to send thousands or millions of emails to the victim's address, quickly filling up their storage quota and causing their email server to crash. Email bombing can disrupt communication, cause data loss, and lead to significant business interruption.

Sniffers are tools used to capture and analyze network traffic. Sniffers can be used legitimately for network troubleshooting and monitoring, but they can also be used maliciously to intercept sensitive data, such as passwords, credit card numbers, and confidential communications. Attackers can deploy sniffers on compromised systems or networks to passively collect data without being detected.

Preventing email bombing and sniffer attacks requires a combination of network security controls, email filtering, and encryption. Rate limiting and connection filtering can help block or slow down email bombing attacks. Email filters can identify and block spam and malicious messages. Encrypting network traffic and email communications can prevent attackers from intercepting sensitive data using sniffers.

Employee training is also crucial for raising awareness about the risks of email bombing and sniffer attacks. Users should be educated about the dangers of opening suspicious emails, clicking on untrusted links, and using unsecured networks. Implementing strong password policies and multi-factor authentication can help protect against credential theft and unauthorized access.

2.12 SOCIAL ENGINEERING, PHARMING, TIMING ATTACK

Social engineering is a type of attack that relies on manipulating human behavior to gain access to systems, data, or physical locations. Social engineers use deception, persuasion, and psychological manipulation to trick victims into divulging sensitive information, installing malware, or granting unauthorized access. Common social engineering tactics include phishing, pretexting, baiting, and quid pro quo.

Pharming is a type of attack that redirects users to fake websites without their knowledge or consent. Pharming attacks typically involve compromising DNS servers or modifying users' host files to redirect traffic to malicious websites that mimic legitimate sites. Pharming can be used to steal login credentials, credit card numbers, and other sensitive information.

Timing attacks exploit vulnerabilities in cryptographic algorithms or protocols to recover secret keys or data. Timing attacks rely on measuring the time it takes to perform certain operations and using that information to infer sensitive data. Timing attacks can be used to compromise encryption keys, authentication tokens, and other security-sensitive information.

Preventing social engineering, pharming, and timing attacks requires a multi-layered approach that includes user education, technical controls, and security policies. Security awareness training can help users recognize and avoid social engineering tactics. Implementing DNS security extensions (DNSSEC) can help prevent DNS poisoning and pharming attacks. Using strong cryptographic algorithms and protocols can help mitigate the risk of timing attacks.

Video Resources

- **What is Intellectual Property?**: https://www.youtube.com/watch?v=fuVqexiDLHg
- **Common Types of Software Exploits**:
  https://www.youtube.com/watch?v=ULvdBPW5PWE
- **QoS Explained**: https://www.youtube.com/watch?v=BJ9EkM92VNo
- **Cyber Espionage**: https://www.youtube.com/watch?v=vWmSvehXA8U
- **Ransomware Explained**: https://www.youtube.com/watch?v=JM_5zF9Szso
- **Cybersecurity Policies and Procedures**:
  https://www.youtube.com/watch?v=M7n4yszYxp4
- **What is Malware?**: https://www.youtube.com/watch?v=qmK06Z0wE-I
- **Password Cracking Explained**:
  https://www.youtube.com/watch?v=9vfMm6fNzos
- **DDoS Explained**: https://www.youtube.com/watch?v=2V43v9oYJOU
- **Man-in-the-Middle Attack**: https://www.youtube.com/watch?v=HltjJmkEA0o
- **Network Sniffing**: https://www.youtube.com/watch?v=V-JmYHm2E1A
- **Social Engineering Explained**: https://www.youtube.com/watch?v=sb39Rq2X-Es
- **Pharming Attack**: https://www.youtube.com/watch?v=e4h1Wj7ZS3g

Use of ICT

ICT plays a vital role in both the execution and mitigation of the cybersecurity threats and attacks outlined in Unit 2. Threat actors leverage ICT to conduct malicious activities such as spreading malware (viruses, worms, trojans), performing phishing attacks, launching DoS/DDoS attacks, conducting man-in-the-middle attacks, and engaging in social engineering. Conversely, security professionals utilize ICT to implement cybersecurity measures such as firewalls, intrusion detection systems (IDS), security information and event management (SIEM), encryption technologies, and access control mechanisms to detect, prevent, and respond to these threats. Regular software updates, vulnerability scanning, and user education through ICT-based platforms are also essential components of a proactive security posture, emphasizing the dual role of ICT in both enabling and defending against cybersecurity risks.

SUMMARY

- **Cybersecurity Threats and Attacks:** Intellectual property theft and software attacks are significant concerns.
- **Cybersecurity Breaches:** Espionage, natural disasters, human error, and information extortion pose substantial risks.
- **Cybersecurity vulnerabilities:** Missing policies and incomplete security controls can lead to sabotage, theft, and system failures.
- **Cybersecurity Malware and Deception:** System affected by Attacks include malicious code, hoaxes, back doors, and password cracking methods.
- **Cybersecurity Operational Disruptions:** Networks Vulnerabilities includes DoS/DDoS, spoofing, man-in-the-middle attacks, spam, email bombing, sniffers, social engineering, pharming, and timing attacks.

EXERCISES

A. Subjective Questions

Category-I (Revised Bloom's Level - 1, 2 & 3): Knowledge, Comprehension, Application

1. Define Intellectual property theft and explain its impact. (Level 1, Knowledge)
2. Describe at least three software attacks. Provide a real-world example for each concept. (Level 2, Comprehension)
3. Explain how and why DoS attack is launched on a computer Network. (Level 2, Comprehension)
4. What are the steps an organization should take to respond to an email bombing attack? (Level 3, Application)
5. Explain the difference between Pharming and Phishing. (Level 2 Comprehension)
6. Describe a situation when Man-in-the-middle attack can be launched. (Level 3 Application)

Category-II (Revised Bloom's Level - 4, 5 & 6): Analysis, Synthesis, Evaluation

1. Analyze the trade-offs between implementing password policies and social engineering attacks. How can an organization effectively balance these competing priorities? (Level 4, Analysis)
2. Design a security awareness training program for employees that addresses phishing attacks and ransomware attacks. (Level 6, Create)
3. Evaluate the effectiveness of different authentication methods (passwords, biometrics, multi-factor authentication) in mitigating brute force attacks. What are the strengths and weaknesses of each? (Level 5, Evaluate)
4. Discuss the ethical implications of using sniffers for identifying fraud or threats. (Level 6, Evaluate)
5. Given a scenario of a security breach due to a DDoS attack, analyze the existing security approaches and design an improved solution to avoid further breaches. (Level 6 Create)

B. Objective Questions

Category-I (Revised Bloom's Level - 1, 2 & 3): Knowledge, Comprehension, Application

1. Which of the following is a loss due to the compromise of Intellectual Property? (Level 1, Knowledge)
   (a) Reputational Loss (b) Productivity Loss
   (c) Financial Loss (d) All of the above

2. Which type of cyber threat involves manipulating a user to click a link in an email to obtain sensitive information? (Level 1, Knowledge)
   (a) Malware (b) Social Engineering
   (c) DoS (d) SQL Injection
3. What is the purpose of a Pharming attack? (Level 2, Comprehension)
   (a) To launch a DDoS Attack (b) To redirect users to a fake website
   (c) To detect malicious activity (d) To steal hardware
4. Which security measure involves monitoring network traffic to obtain credentials or perform malicious activities? (Level 2, Comprehension)
   (a) Firewall (b) Antivirus Software
   (c) Sniffer (d) Email Bomber

Category-II *(Revised Bloom's Level - 4, 5 & 6): Analysis, Synthesis, Evaluation*

1. Which of the following attacks would be most effective in preventing a breach when a good firewall is in place? (Level 5, Evaluation)
   (a) Phishing (b) Denial Of Service
   (c) SQL injection (d) Virus
2. Which security principle is most directly violated by a denial-of-service (DoS) attack? (Level 4, Analysis)
   (a) Confidentiality (b) Integrity
   (c) Availability (d) Non-repudiation
3. Which of the following methods would BEST stop a password cracking attack? (Level 5, Evaluation)
   (a) Encryption (b) Access Controls
   (c) Multi Factor Authentication (d) Hashing Algorithms
4. An organisation wants to ensure that it can classify whether the user is a bot or a real user, which approach is best to follow to stop brute force attacks. (Level 5, Application)
   (a) Use of CAPTCHA (b) Business Continuity Plan
   (c) Vulnerability assesment (d) Patch management

TEACHER'S KNOW MORE

To deepen student understanding of cybersecurity threats and attacks, educators should emphasize the interconnectedness of different threat vectors, illustrating how a single vulnerability, like a missing security patch, can be exploited through multiple attack methods such as malware injection or social engineering; furthermore, real-world case studies of significant data breaches and cyberattacks, highlighting the financial, reputational, and operational consequences for organizations, can effectively demonstrate the tangible impact of these threats; it is also helpful to introduce the concept of threat actors, discussing their motivations, capabilities, and common tactics, to provide students with a more comprehensive perspective on the threat landscape; additionally, hands-on activities such as simulated phishing exercises or vulnerability scanning can enhance practical skills, reinforcing the importance of proactive security measures and continuous monitoring in mitigating cyber risks and protecting digital assets.

3 UNIT

Security Tools & Technologies

RATIONALE

A chapter dedicated to Security Tools & Technologies is crucial within a cybersecurity curriculum because it bridges theoretical understanding with practical application, equipping students with the knowledge and skills to implement and manage essential security defenses. Covering firewalls and VPNs, intrusion detection and prevention systems, access control mechanisms, and specialized systems like honeypots provides a holistic view of the tools available to protect networks and data. Furthermore, addressing the specific challenges of securing remote connections prepares students for the realities of modern work environments. By exploring these tools and technologies, students gain a deeper appreciation for the complexity of cybersecurity and develop the ability to design, deploy, and maintain effective security solutions.

UNIT OUTCOMES

- Understand firewall and VPN technologies to secure network communications.
- Deploy Intrusion Detection and Prevention Systems to identify and mitigate network threats.
- Classify and select appropriate security tools for various organizational needs.
- Implement access control mechanisms to protect sensitive data and resources.
- Evaluate and utilize honeypots and honeynets to gather threat intelligence.

3.1 FIREWALLS AND VPNs

Firewalls and Virtual Private Networks (VPNs) are foundational security tools for protecting networks and data. A firewall acts as a barrier between a trusted internal network and untrusted external networks, such as the internet. It examines network traffic based on predefined rules, blocking or allowing packets based on their source, destination, protocol, and port number. Firewalls can be implemented as hardware appliances, software applications, or a combination of both, providing a critical first line of defense against unauthorized access and malicious activity.

Modern firewalls often incorporate advanced features such as intrusion detection and prevention, application control, and web filtering, providing a comprehensive security solution. Next-Generation Firewalls (NGFWs) offer even greater capabilities, including deep packet inspection, malware detection, and integration with threat intelligence feeds. These advanced features enable organizations to better protect against sophisticated cyberattacks and maintain a strong security posture. Figure 3.1 illustrates the working of a Firewall.

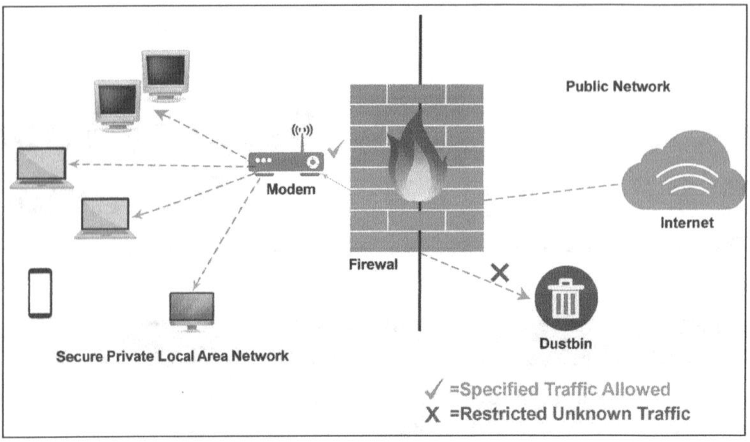

Figure 3.1: *How does a Firewall Work*

Types of Firewalls

1. Packet Filtering Firewalls

Packet filtering firewalls as given in figure 3.2 are the most basic type of firewall, operating by examining individual packets and making decisions based on a set of rules. These rules typically involve checking the source and destination IP addresses, port numbers, and protocols. If a packet matches a rule that allows traffic, it's permitted through; otherwise, it's blocked. Packet filtering is fast and relatively simple to implement, making it a cost-effective option for basic network security. However, their limited inspection capabilities mean they can be vulnerable to more sophisticated attacks that can spoof IP addresses or hide malicious content within seemingly legitimate packets.

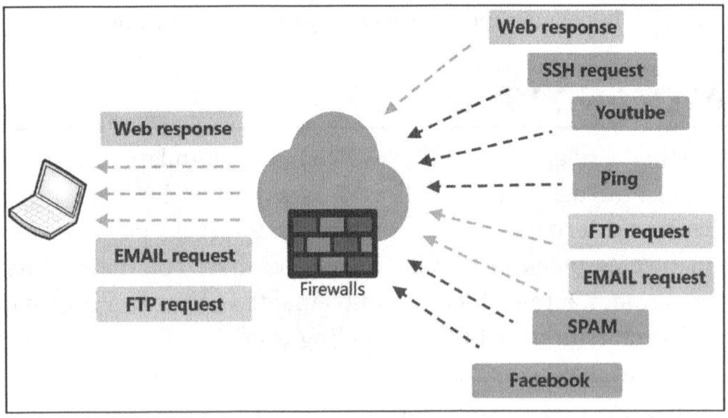

Figure 3.2: *Packet Filtering Firewalls*

2. Stateful Inspection Firewalls

Taking security a step further, stateful inspection firewalls as given in figure 3.3 track the state of network connections. They not only examine the packet header but also analyze the context of the connection, ensuring that traffic is part of an established, authorized session. This allows them to identify and block traffic that appears to be part of a new, unauthorized connection attempt, even if the packets themselves seem legitimate. Stateful inspection is more secure than simple packet filtering, as it can detect and prevent certain types of attacks, such as TCP SYN floods, but it also requires more processing power and can be more complex to configure.

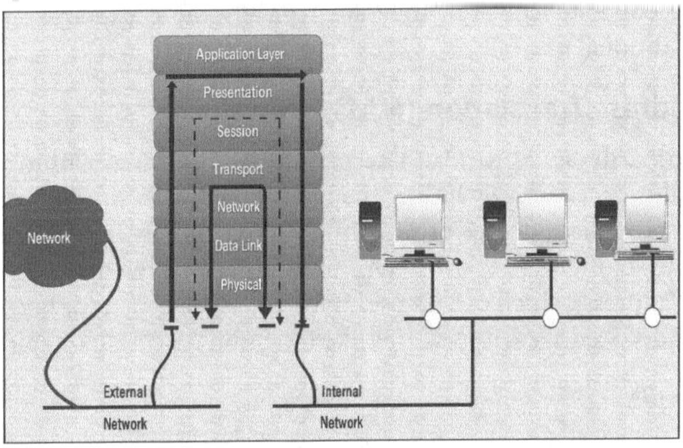

Figure 3.3: *Stateful Inspection Firewalls*

3. Proxy Firewalls (Application-Layer Firewalls)

Proxy firewalls, also known as application-layer firewalls, act as intermediaries between clients and servers. All traffic is proxied through the firewall, which examines the application-layer data (e.g., HTTP, SMTP). Instead of directly connecting to the destination server, the client connects to the proxy firewall, which then forwards the request to the server on the client's behalf. This allows the firewall to inspect the actual content of the traffic and apply application-specific security rules. Proxy firewalls as given in figure 3.4 offer a high level of security but can introduce latency due to the overhead of proxying traffic.

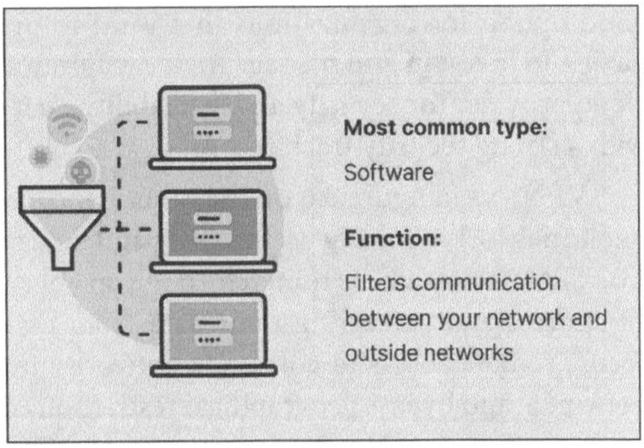

Figure 3.4: *Proxy Firewalls*

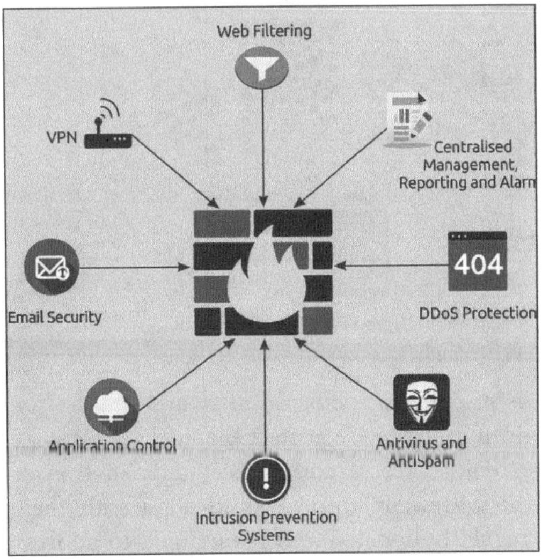

Figure 3.5: *Next Generation Firewalls*

4. Next-Generation Firewalls (NGFWs)

Next-generation firewalls (NGFWs) as shown in figure 3.5 represent a significant evolution in firewall technology. They combine traditional firewall features with advanced security capabilities, such as intrusion prevention systems (IPS), application control, deep packet inspection (DPI), and malware filtering. NGFWs offer comprehensive security protection against a wide range of threats, allowing organizations to identify and block malicious traffic based on application type, user identity, and content. However, they are typically more expensive and complex to configure than traditional firewalls.

5. Network Address Translation (NAT) Firewalls

NAT firewalls primarily serve to translate private IP addresses within a network to a single public IP address, effectively hiding the internal network structure from the outside world. While this provides a degree of security by obscuring internal IP addresses, it's not a complete security solution on its own. NAT firewalls also allow multiple devices to share a single public IP address, which can be useful for conserving IP addresses. However, they may not provide advanced security features like intrusion detection or application control.

6. Cloud Firewalls

Cloud firewalls are delivered as a service from a cloud provider, offering the same functionality as traditional firewalls but with the added benefits of scalability, cost-effectiveness, and ease of deployment. These firewalls are managed and maintained by the cloud provider, reducing the burden on the organization's IT staff. Cloud firewalls are a good option for organizations that want to protect their cloud-based resources without having to invest in and manage their own firewall infrastructure. However, they rely on the cloud provider for security and availability, so it's important to choose a reputable provider with a strong security track record.

VPNs, as in figure 3.6 on the other hand, create a secure, encrypted connection over a public network, allowing users to transmit data privately and securely. When a user connects to a VPN, their traffic is routed through an encrypted tunnel to a VPN server, masking their IP address and protecting their data from eavesdropping. VPNs are commonly used to secure remote access to corporate networks, protect against surveillance on public Wi-Fi networks, and bypass geographical restrictions on content.

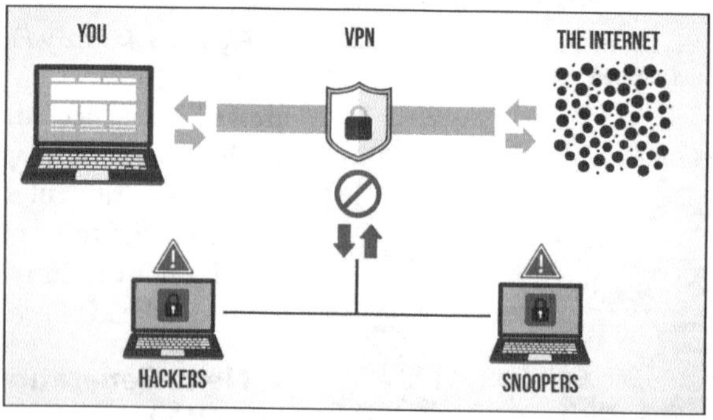

***Figure 3.6:** VPN*

The combination of firewalls and VPNs provides a robust security architecture for protecting networks and data. Firewalls as given in figure 3.1 protect the internal network from external threats, while VPNs secure remote access and protect data in transit. Organizations should carefully configure their firewalls and VPNs to align with their security policies and ensure that they are regularly updated and maintained to address emerging threats.

In summary, firewalls and VPNs are essential security tools for protecting networks and data in today's interconnected world. Firewalls act as a barrier between trusted and untrusted networks, while VPNs provide secure, encrypted connections for remote access and data transmission. By implementing and properly configuring these technologies, organizations can significantly reduce their risk of falling victim to cyberattacks and protect their critical assets.

3.2 INTRUSION DETECTION AND PREVENTION SYSTEMS (IDS/IPS)

Intrusion Detection Systems (IDS) and Intrusion Prevention Systems (IPS) are critical components of a comprehensive security strategy, designed to identify and respond to malicious activity within a network or system. An IDS passively monitors network traffic and system logs for suspicious patterns, anomalies, and policy violations, generating alerts when potential threats are detected. An IPS, on the other hand, takes a more active role by automatically blocking or mitigating malicious traffic and activities, preventing attacks from reaching their intended targets.

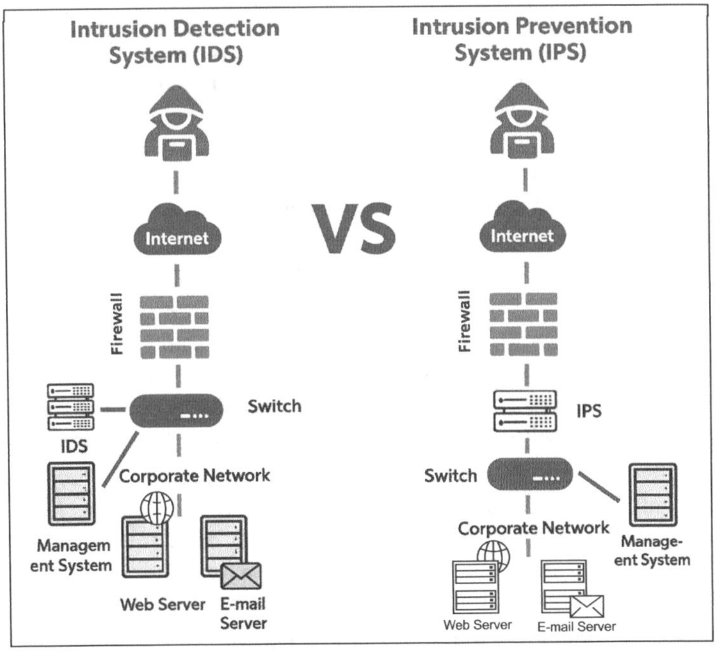

Figure 3.7: *IDS vs IPS*

Figure 3.7 gives IDS vs IPS. IDS and IPS solutions employ various detection techniques, including signature-based detection, anomaly-based detection, and behavior-based detection. Signature-based detection relies on pre-defined patterns of known attacks to identify malicious activity, while anomaly-based detection identifies deviations from normal behavior that may indicate a threat. Behavior-based detection analyzes the actions of users and applications to identify suspicious or malicious behavior.

The effectiveness of an IDS/IPS depends on its ability to accurately detect and respond to threats without generating excessive false positives. False positives can overwhelm security teams with alerts, making it difficult to identify genuine threats. Tuning and configuration are essential for optimizing the performance of an IDS/IPS and minimizing false positives. Organizations should regularly review and update their IDS/IPS rules and policies to reflect the evolving threat landscape.

Modern IDS/IPS solutions often integrate with other security tools and technologies, such as firewalls, SIEM systems, and threat intelligence feeds, to provide a more comprehensive security posture. Integration with threat intelligence feeds enables the IDS/IPS to identify and block known malicious IP addresses, domains, and URLs. SIEM integration provides centralized logging and analysis capabilities, allowing security teams to correlate alerts from multiple sources and gain a more complete understanding of security incidents.

In conclusion, Intrusion Detection and Prevention Systems are essential security tools for identifying and responding to malicious activity within a network or system. By passively monitoring traffic for malicious activity or actively blocking such traffic, organizations can significantly reduce their risk of falling victim to cyberattacks and protect their critical assets. Effective use of IDS/IPS requires careful tuning and configuration, regular updates, and integration with other security tools and technologies.

3.3 OTHER SECURITY TOOLS, ACCESS CONTROL, FIREWALLS

Beyond firewalls and intrusion detection systems, a comprehensive security strategy relies on a diverse array of other security tools, each designed to address specific threats and vulnerabilities. These tools include vulnerability scanners, penetration testing tools, anti-malware software, data loss prevention (DLP) solutions, and security information and event management (SIEM) systems. Each tool plays a unique role in strengthening the overall security posture.

Access control mechanisms are fundamental for restricting access to sensitive data and resources, ensuring that only authorized individuals can perform specific actions. Access control lists (ACLs) define the permissions granted to users and groups, while role-based access control (RBAC) assigns permissions based on job roles and responsibilities. Multi-factor authentication (MFA) adds an extra layer of security by requiring users to provide multiple forms of identification, such as a password and a one-time code.

Firewalls, as previously discussed, are essential for controlling network traffic and preventing unauthorized access. They can be configured to block specific IP addresses, ports, and protocols, as well as to filter traffic based on content. Modern firewalls often incorporate advanced features such as intrusion detection and prevention, application control, and web filtering, providing a comprehensive security solution.

Data Loss Prevention (DLP) solutions are designed to prevent sensitive data from leaving the organization's control. DLP tools can monitor network traffic, email communications, and file storage systems to detect and block the transmission of sensitive data, such as credit card numbers, social security numbers, and confidential business information. DLP can help organizations comply with data privacy regulations and protect against data breaches.

Security Information and Event Management (SIEM) systems provide centralized logging and analysis capabilities, allowing security teams to monitor and analyze security events from multiple sources. SIEM systems can correlate alerts from different security tools to identify patterns and trends, providing valuable insights into potential security incidents. SIEM systems also support compliance reporting and auditing.

3.4 PROTECTING REMOTE CONNECTIONS

Protecting remote connections is crucial for organizations that allow employees to work remotely or access corporate resources from outside the office. Remote connections can create significant security risks if not properly secured, as they bypass traditional network perimeter defenses. Several technologies and best practices can be employed to protect remote connections and minimize the risk of unauthorized access and data breaches.

Virtual Private Networks (VPNs) are commonly used to secure remote connections, creating an encrypted tunnel between the remote device and the corporate network. VPNs protect data in transit from eavesdropping and ensure that only authorized users can access corporate resources. Strong authentication mechanisms, such as multi-factor authentication, should be used in conjunction with VPNs to verify the identity of remote users.

Remote Desktop Protocol (RDP) is another technology used to access remote systems, but it can be a significant security risk if not properly secured. RDP is a common target for attackers, who often exploit vulnerabilities in RDP implementations to gain unauthorized access to systems. Organizations should disable RDP if it is not needed, or implement strong security controls to protect RDP connections, such as restricting access to specific IP addresses and using strong passwords.

Secure Shell (SSH) is a secure protocol used to remotely access and manage systems. SSH provides encryption and authentication, protecting data in transit from eavesdropping and ensuring that only authorized users can access systems. SSH should be used in place of Telnet, which is an unencrypted protocol that transmits data in clear text.

Endpoint security solutions can help protect remote devices from malware and other threats. Endpoint security solutions typically include antivirus software, firewalls, intrusion detection systems, and data loss prevention capabilities. These solutions can help prevent remote devices from being compromised and used to attack the corporate network.

3.5 HONEYPOTS, HONEYNETS, AND PADDED CELL SYSTEMS

Honeypots, honeynets, and padded cell systems are security tools designed to deceive and trap attackers, providing valuable insights into their tactics, techniques, and procedures (TTPs). These systems act as decoys, attracting attackers away from valuable assets and allowing security teams to study their behavior in a controlled environment. Honeypots as represented in figure 3.8 are typically isolated systems or applications that appear vulnerable and contain enticing data.

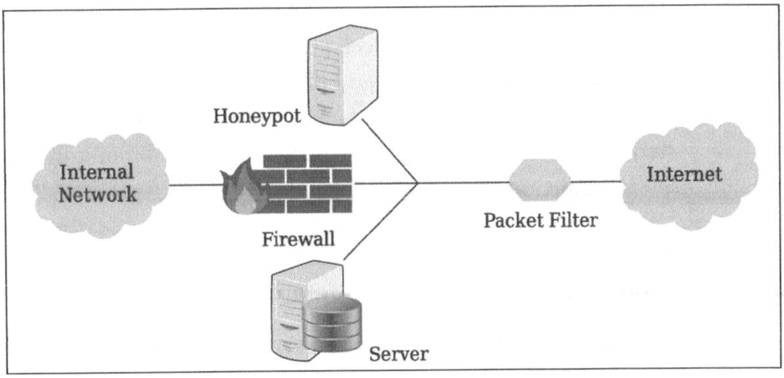

Figure 3.8: *Honeypot*

Honeynets as represented in figure 3.9 are networks of honeypots, designed to simulate a real network environment and attract more sophisticated attackers. Honeynets can provide a more comprehensive view of attacker behavior, allowing security teams to study their movement within the network and the tools they use. Honeynets are often used for research and development purposes, helping security professionals understand the latest attack techniques and develop more effective defenses.

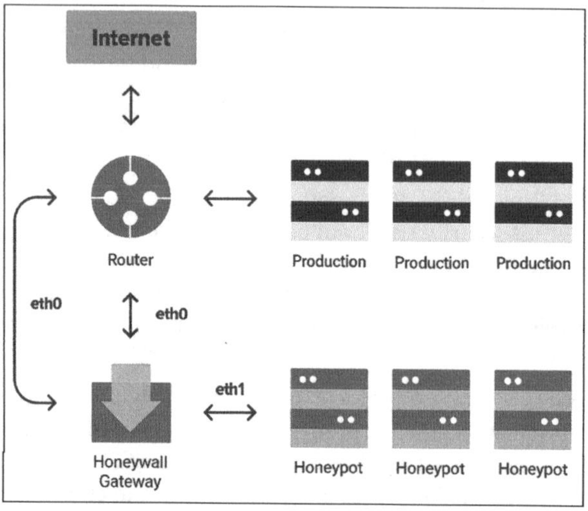

***Figure 3.9:** Honeynet*

Padded cell systems are similar to honeypots, but they are designed to contain and isolate attackers, preventing them from reaching other systems on the network. Padded cell systems typically include security controls that restrict the attacker's movements and limit their ability to cause damage. Padded cell systems can be used to gather intelligence about attackers and their methods, as well as to prevent them from compromising critical assets.

The data collected from honeypots, honeynets, and padded cell systems can be used to improve security defenses, develop new detection signatures, and train security personnel. By studying attacker behavior, security teams can gain a better understanding of the threats they face and develop more effective strategies for mitigating those threats. The intelligence gathered from these systems can also be shared with the broader security community, helping to improve overall cybersecurity awareness and defenses.

While honeypots, honeynets, and padded cell systems can be valuable security tools, they also carry some risks. If not properly configured and monitored, these systems can be compromised and used to attack other systems. Security teams should carefully plan and implement these systems, ensuring that they are properly isolated and monitored to prevent them from being used for malicious purposes.

Video Resources

- **Firewall and VPNs:** https://www.youtube.com/watch?v=1_jKbmC9cBc
- **Intrusion Detection and Prevention Systems:** https://www.youtube.com/watch?v=V0J3xlJ8BSk

- **Other Security Tools, Access Control :** https://www.youtube.com/watch?v=916vTw9U7xw
- **Protecting Remote Connections:** https://www.youtube.com/watch?v=r7JwMzE_VWI –
- **Honeypots, Honeynets and Padded Cell Systems:** https://www.youtube.com/watch?v=hF3rkmEQD0w

Use of ICT

ICT plays a vital role in both the execution and mitigation of the cybersecurity threats and attacks outlined in Unit 2. Threat actors leverage ICT to conduct malicious activities such as spreading malware (viruses, worms, trojans), performing phishing attacks, launching DoS/DDoS attacks, conducting man-in-the-middle attacks, and engaging in social engineering. Conversely, security professionals utilize ICT to implement cybersecurity measures such as firewalls, intrusion detection systems (IDS), security information and event management (SIEM), encryption technologies, and access control mechanisms to detect, prevent, and respond to these threats. Regular software updates, vulnerability scanning, and user education through ICT-based platforms are also essential components of a proactive security posture, emphasizing the dual role of ICT in both enabling and defending against cybersecurity risks.

SUMMARY

- Firewalls act as a critical barrier, controlling network traffic based on security rules to prevent unauthorized access.
- VPNs establish secure, encrypted connections for remote users, protecting data transmitted over public networks.
- Intrusion Detection Systems (IDS) monitor network traffic for malicious activity, while Intrusion Prevention Systems (IPS) actively block detected threats.
- Vulnerability scanners identify weaknesses in systems and applications, helping organizations proactively address security flaws.
- Access control mechanisms, like RBAC and MFA, restrict access to sensitive resources, ensuring only authorized users gain entry.
- Protecting remote connections involves using VPNs, strong authentication, and endpoint security solutions to secure devices outside the network perimeter.
- Honeypots are decoy systems that attract attackers, allowing security teams to study their methods and gather threat intelligence.
- Honeynets extend the concept of honeypots by creating entire decoy networks, simulating a real environment to observe attacker behavior on a larger scale.
- Padded cell systems isolate attackers, preventing them from reaching critical systems while allowing security teams to analyze their actions.
- Effective use of security tools and technologies requires ongoing monitoring, regular updates, and integration with security policies and incident response plans.

EXERCISES

A. Subjective Questions

Category-I (Revised Bloom's Level - 1, 2 & 3): Knowledge, Comprehension, Application

1. Define what a firewall is and explain its purpose in network security. (Level 1, Knowledge)
2. Describe how a VPN protects remote connections. Give examples of when a VPN can be used. (Level 2, Comprehension; Level 3, Application)
3. Explain how an Intrusion Detection System (IDS) differs from an Intrusion Prevention System (IPS). (Level 2, Comprehension)
4. Outline three different methods that can be used to implement access control. (Level 2, Comprehension)
5. Describe how a padded cell system isolates attackers in a network. What is the end goal? (Level 1, Knowledge; Level 2, Comprehension)

Category-II *(Revised Bloom's Level - 4, 5 & 6): Analysis, Synthesis, Evaluation*

1. Analyze the trade-offs between security and usability when implementing multi-factor authentication. (Level 4, Analysis)
2. Design a network security plan for a small business that incorporates firewalls, VPNs, and an intrusion detection system. (Level 6, Create)
3. Evaluate the effectiveness of honeypots and honeynets as security tools. What are the ethical considerations? (Level 5, Evaluate)
4. Given a scenario where a company experiences a data breach due to a compromised remote connection, analyze the likely security gaps and recommend improvements. (Level 4, Analysis; Level 6, Create)
5. Compare and contrast the use of signature-based detection versus anomaly-based detection in an intrusion prevention system. (Level 5, Evaluate)

B. Objective Questions

Category-I *(Revised Bloom's Level - 1, 2 & 3): Knowledge, Comprehension, Application*

1. Which of the following is a primary function of a firewall? (Level 1, Knowledge)
   (a) Encrypting data (b) Monitoring network traffic
   (c) Blocking unauthorized access (d) Preventing malware infections
2. What type of connection does a VPN create? (Level 1, Knowledge)
   (a) An open, unencrypted connection (b) A direct physical connection
   (c) A secure, encrypted connection (d) A wireless connection

3. An Intrusion Prevention System (IPS) primarily functions to: (Level 2, Comprehension)
   (a) Detect but not block malicious traffic
   (b) Log all network activity
   (c) Actively block or prevent malicious traffic
   (d) Encrypt network data
4. Which of the following access control methods is based on job roles? (Level 1, Knowledge)
   (a) Mandatory Access Control (MAC)
   (b) Discretionary Access Control (DAC)
   (c) Role-Based Access Control (RBAC)
   (d) Rule-Based Access Control
5. What is the primary purpose of a honeypot? (Level 2, Comprehension)
   (a) To protect sensitive data
   (b) To filter network traffic
   (c) To attract and trap attackers
   (d) To encrypt communications

Category-II (Revised Bloom's Level - 4, 5 & 6): Analysis, Synthesis, Evaluation

1. Which of the following scenarios would best justify the use of a honeynet over a single honeypot? (Level 5, Evaluate)
   (a) Protecting a small home network
   (b) Analyzing the behavior of advanced persistent threats (APTs)
   (c) Detecting basic port scanning activity
   (d) Encrypting sensitive data
2. A company wants to implement a solution that not only detects but also automatically blocks malicious network traffic. Which of the following is the MOST suitable choice? (Level 5, Evaluate)
   (a) Firewall
   (b) Intrusion Detection System (IDS)
   (c) Intrusion Prevention System (IPS)
   (d) Vulnerability Scanner
3. Which of the following security measures BEST addresses the risk of unauthorized access from a compromised laptop used remotely? (Level 5, Evaluate)
   (a) Disabling the laptop's firewall
   (b) Implementing multi-factor authentication (MFA)
   (c) Installing more RAM on the laptop
   (d) Allowing unrestricted access to the network
4. An organization has implemented a strong firewall and an intrusion detection system. What additional security tool would MOST enhance their ability to analyze and respond to security incidents? (Level 5, Evaluate)
   (a) Data Loss Prevention (DLP) system
   (b) Security Information and Event Management (SIEM) system

(c) Vulnerability Scanner
(d) Password Manager

5. An organization needs to balance highly secure remote access with ease of use for its employees. Which approach BEST achieves this balance? (Level 6, Evaluate)
(a) Requiring complex passwords that are changed daily
(b) Implementing multi-factor authentication (MFA) with biometric login
(c) Disabling remote access entirely
(d) Allowing unrestricted access with no security measures

TEACHER'S KNOW MORE

Teachers should understand that firewalls and VPNs are fundamental network security tools: firewalls act as a barrier controlling network traffic, while VPNs secure remote connections. They need to grasp the role of Intrusion Detection and Prevention Systems (IDS/IPS) in identifying and mitigating malicious activities. Furthermore, they should be aware of other security tools like honeypots, honeynets, and padded cell systems that lure and trap attackers to gather intelligence. Access control mechanisms, including role-based access control (RBAC) and multi-factor authentication (MFA), are crucial for limiting access to sensitive resources. A comprehensive understanding of these components is essential for explaining layered security approaches and the importance of protecting digital assets.

4 UNIT Cryptography

RATIONALE

A book chapter focused on cryptography is essential for any comprehensive cybersecurity curriculum because it provides the foundational knowledge necessary for understanding modern data protection and secure communication. Covering cryptology terminology establishes a common language and understanding of core concepts. Exploring various cipher methods illuminates the evolution of encryption techniques and their underlying principles. A thorough examination of cryptographic algorithms equips readers with the ability to select and implement appropriate encryption solutions. Furthermore, addressing cryptographic tools provides practical insights into applying cryptographic principles in real-world scenarios. Discussing attacks on cryptosystems is crucial for understanding the limitations of cryptographic solutions and the importance of robust key management and implementation practices. Finally, addressing physical security highlights the often-overlooked importance of protecting cryptographic systems from physical threats, ensuring a holistic understanding of cryptographic security. By addressing these topics, the chapter empowers readers to build, maintain, and analyze secure systems in an increasingly hostile digital landscape.

UNIT OUTCOMES

- Master cryptology terminology to effectively communicate about cryptographic concepts and techniques.
- Apply various cipher methods to encrypt and decrypt data, understanding their strengths and weaknesses.
- Select and implement appropriate cryptographic algorithms for specific security requirements.
- Utilize cryptographic tools for key generation, digital signatures, and secure communication.
- Analyze attacks on cryptosystems to identify vulnerabilities and implement countermeasures.
- Apply physical security principles to protect cryptographic systems and prevent unauthorized access.

4.1 CRYPTOLOGY TERMINOLOGY

Cryptology, the science of secure communication, relies on a specialized vocabulary to ensure precise understanding and implementation. At its core, cryptology encompasses both cryptography and cryptanalysis. Cryptography is the art of designing ciphers, algorithms used to encrypt and decrypt messages, while cryptanalysis focuses on breaking those ciphers, revealing the underlying plaintext without authorization. Understanding these two branches is essential for anyone working in the field of secure communication.

Within cryptography, key terms include plaintext, the original message to be protected, and ciphertext, the scrambled version of the plaintext produced by encryption. Encryption is the process of converting plaintext to ciphertext, while decryption reverses this process, transforming ciphertext back into readable plaintext. The key, a secret piece of information used by both the encryption and decryption algorithms, is paramount for secure communication. Without the correct key, deciphering the ciphertext becomes significantly more challenging, if not impossible.

Beyond these fundamental terms, other crucial concepts include algorithms, which are the step-by-step procedures used for encryption and decryption. Symmetric-key algorithms use the same key for both encryption and decryption, while asymmetric-key algorithms employ a pair of keys: a public key for encryption and a private key for decryption. Hash functions as given in figure 4.1 is another vital component, are one-way functions that produce a fixed-size output (hash) from an input of any size, used for verifying data integrity.

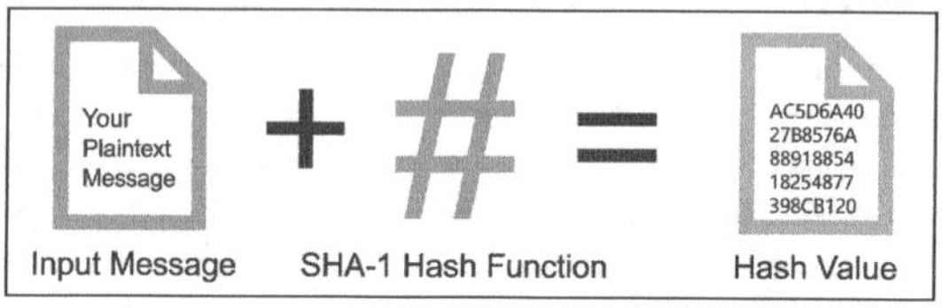

Figure 4.1: *An Example of a Hash Function*

Steganography, a related but distinct field, focuses on concealing the existence of a message rather than encrypting its content. This involves embedding the message within an innocuous carrier, such as an image or audio file, making it difficult to detect the presence of secret communication. Together, these terms and concepts form the foundation for understanding the principles and practices of modern cryptology.

Finally, understanding the different types of attacks against cryptosystems is crucial. These include ciphertext-only attacks, where the attacker only has access to ciphertext; known-plaintext attacks, where the attacker has access to both plaintext and corresponding ciphertext; chosen-plaintext attacks, where the attacker can choose the plaintext to be encrypted; and chosen-ciphertext attacks, where the attacker can choose the ciphertext to be decrypted. Recognizing these attack models informs the design and selection of robust cryptographic algorithms and protocols.

4.2 CIPHER METHODS

Cipher methods are the techniques used to transform plaintext into ciphertext, concealing the original message from unauthorized eyes. These methods range from simple substitution ciphers to complex mathematical algorithms, each offering varying degrees of security. The choice of cipher method depends on the level of security required, the computational resources available, and the specific application.

One of the earliest and simplest cipher methods is the substitution cipher, where each letter of the plaintext is replaced with another letter, number, or symbol. The Caesar cipher, a well-known example, shifts each letter a fixed number of positions down the alphabet. While easy to implement, substitution ciphers are vulnerable to frequency analysis, where attackers exploit the statistical distribution of letters in the language to break the code.

Here's a mathematical example illustrating two common cipher methods, the **Caesar Cipher** and the **Diffie-Hellman Key Exchange**.

Caesar Cipher (Substitution Cipher)

The Caesar Cipher is a simple substitution cipher where each letter in the plaintext is shifted by a fixed number of positions in the alphabet.

Example

- **Plaintext**: HELLO
- **Key**: 3 (shift each letter by 3 positions)
- **Encryption**:
  - ✓ H → K
  - ✓ E → H
  - ✓ L → O
  - ✓ L → O
  - ✓ O → R
- **Ciphertext**: KHOOR

To decrypt, shift each letter back by the same key (3 in this case).

Diffie-Hellman Key Exchange (Asymmetric Encryption)

This is a method for two parties to securely share a secret key over an insecure channel.

Example

1. **Public Parameters**:
   - ✓ Prime number p=29
   - ✓ Base g=5
2. **Private Keys**:
   - ✓ Bob chooses x=4
   - ✓ Alice chooses y=8
3. **Compute Public Keys**:
   - Bob computes X= g^x mod p = 5^4 mod 29 = 625 mod 29 = 16
   - Alice computes Y=g^y mod p = 5^8 mod 29 = 390625 mod 29 = 24
4. **Exchange Public Keys**:
   - Bob sends X=16 to Alice.
   - Alice sends Y=24 to Bob.
4. **Compute Shared Secret**:
   - Bob computes K=Y^x mod p = 24^4 mod 29 = 331776 mod 29 = 16
   - Alice computes K=X^y mod p = 16^8 mod 29 = 4294967296 mod 29 = 16

Both Bob and Alice now share the same secret key K=16 which can be used for encryption and decryption.

Transposition ciphers, on the other hand, rearrange the order of the plaintext letters without substituting them. This can involve writing the message in a grid and reading it out in a different order, or using a more complex permutation algorithm. Transposition ciphers can be combined with substitution ciphers to create stronger encryption schemes.

Modern cipher methods rely on complex mathematical algorithms and computer technology to achieve high levels of security. These algorithms operate on binary data rather than individual letters, and they use keys to control the encryption and decryption processes. Block ciphers, such as AES (Advanced Encryption Standard), divide the plaintext into fixed-size blocks and encrypt each block independently. Stream ciphers, such as RC4, encrypt the plaintext one byte or bit at a time, using a key stream generated from a seed value.

The effectiveness of a cipher method depends on its resistance to various types of attacks. Brute-force attacks attempt to try every possible key until the correct one is found, while cryptanalytic attacks exploit weaknesses in the algorithm to deduce the key or recover the plaintext. A strong cipher method should be resistant to both brute-force and cryptanalytic attacks, and it should have a key space large enough to make brute-force attacks computationally infeasible.

4.3 CRYPTOGRAPHIC ALGORITHMS

Cryptographic algorithms are the mathematical procedures that form the backbone of modern secure communication. They provide the means to encrypt and decrypt data, ensuring confidentiality, integrity, and authenticity. These algorithms are classified into symmetric-key algorithms, asymmetric-key algorithms, and hash functions, each with distinct properties and applications.

Symmetric-key algorithms, also known as secret-key algorithms, use the same key for both encryption and decryption. This makes them fast and efficient, suitable for encrypting large amounts of data. Popular symmetric-key algorithms include AES (Advanced Encryption Standard), DES (Data Encryption Standard), and Triple DES. However, the security of symmetric-key algorithms depends on keeping the key secret, which can be a challenge in distributed environments.

Asymmetric-key algorithms, also known as public-key algorithms, use a pair of keys: a public key for encryption and a private key for decryption. The public key can be freely distributed, allowing anyone to encrypt messages for the owner of the corresponding private key. Only the owner of the private key can decrypt the messages, ensuring confidentiality. Asymmetric-key algorithms are also used for digital signatures, where the private key is used to sign a message, and the public key is used to verify the signature. Popular asymmetric-key algorithms include RSA, ECC (Elliptic Curve Cryptography), and Diffie-Hellman.

Hash functions are one-way functions that take an input of any size and produce a fixed-size output, called a hash. Hash functions are designed to be collision-resistant, meaning that it is computationally infeasible to find two different inputs that produce the same hash value. Hash functions are used for verifying data integrity, creating digital signatures, and storing passwords securely. Popular hash functions include SHA-256, SHA-3, and MD5 (though MD5 is now considered insecure for many applications).

The selection of a cryptographic algorithm depends on the specific security requirements of the application. Symmetric-key algorithms are suitable for encrypting large amounts of data when speed is a priority, while asymmetric-key algorithms are suitable for secure key exchange and digital signatures. Hash functions are used for verifying data integrity and storing passwords securely. Understanding the strengths and weaknesses of different cryptographic algorithms is essential for designing secure systems.

Example: AES Encryption Algorithm (Simplified)

Input:

- Plaintext (128-bit block)
- Encryption Key (128, 192, or 256 bits)

Steps:

1. **Key Expansion**
   - Derive a set of round keys from the encryption key using a key schedule algorithm. The number of round keys depends on the key size (10 rounds for 128-bit keys, 12 rounds for 192-bit keys, and 14 rounds for 256-bit keys).
2. **Initial Round**
   - **Add Round Key:** XOR the plaintext block with the first round key.

3. **Main Rounds (Repeat for the number of rounds)**
   - **Substitute Bytes (SubBytes):** Replace each byte in the state matrix with a corresponding byte from a substitution box (S-box). This is a non-linear byte substitution.
   - **Shift Rows (ShiftRows):** Cyclically shift the rows of the state matrix to the left. Each row is shifted by a different offset.
   - **Mix Columns (MixColumns):** Perform a mixing operation on the columns of the state matrix. This step is skipped in the last round.
   - **Add Round Key:** XOR the state matrix with the appropriate round key for that round.
4. **Final Round**
   - **Substitute Bytes (SubBytes):** Same as in the main rounds.
   - **Shift Rows (ShiftRows):** Same as in the main rounds.
   - **Add Round Key:** XOR the state matrix with the last round key.
5. **Output:** The resulting state matrix is the ciphertext (128-bit block).

Explanation of Steps

- **Key Expansion:** The original key is used to generate multiple round keys, ensuring each round uses a different key.
- **Add Round Key:** Combines the round key with the state (the data being processed) using XOR.
- **SubBytes:** Provides non-linearity, confusing the relationship between the key and the ciphertext.
- **ShiftRows:** Provides diffusion, spreading the influence of each input bit across the output.
- **MixColumns:** Provides further diffusion, ensuring that changes in one byte affect multiple bytes in the next round.

Table 4.1: Comparison of different types of cryptographic algorithms.

Algorithm Type	Examples	Key Type	Use Cases	Advantages	Disadvantages
Symmetric-Key	AES, 3DES, DES	Single shared key	Data encryption, message authentication	Fast and efficient	Requires secure key exchange
Asymmetric-Key	RSA, ECC, Diffie-Hellman	Public and private keys	Digital signatures, key exchange	No need to share private key	Slower than symmetric algorithms
Hash Functions	SHA-256, MD5	No key	Data integrity, password storage	One-way process, ensures data integrity	Cannot be reversed; vulnerable to collisions

Algorithm Type	Examples	Key Type	Use Cases	Advantages	Disadvantages
Stream Ciphers	RC4	Single shared key	Real-time encryption (e.g., video streams)	Low latency	Vulnerable if key reuse occurs
Post-Quantum	Lattice-based, Multivariate Polynomials	Public and private keys	Future-proof encryption	Resistant to quantum attacks	Still under research and standardization

The table 4.1 summarizes the strengths and weaknesses of major cryptographic algorithm types based on their structure and applications.

4.4 CRYPTOGRAPHIC TOOLS

Cryptographic tools encompass a wide array of hardware and software solutions that enable the implementation and management of cryptographic algorithms and protocols. These tools range from command-line utilities to comprehensive security platforms, each offering specific functionalities for encryption, decryption, key management, and digital signatures. Selecting the right cryptographic tools is crucial for building secure systems and protecting sensitive data.

Table 4.2: Detailed comparison of different cryptographic tools in a table format.

Tool Name	Type	Key Features	Use Cases	Advantages	Disadvantages
VeraCrypt	Symmetric Encryption	Open-source, automatic data encryption, supports multiple OS	Disk encryption, secure file storage	Easy to use, robust encryption	Limited updates in free version
Kruptos 2	Symmetric Encryption	256-bit AES encryption, cross-platform compatibility	File and cloud encryption	Strong password generator	Not suitable for large-scale enterprise use
Boxcryptor	Hybrid (AES + RSA)	End-to-end encryption for over 30 cloud services	Cloud-based file security	Intuitive interface, multi-device support	Requires subscription for advanced features
IBM Security Guardium	Enterprise Encryption	Centralized key management, granular data protection	Enterprise-level data encryption	Compliance-ready libraries	High cost
CertMgr.exe	Certificate Management	Manages encryption certificates and revocation lists	Secure certificate-based communication	Simplifies certificate management	Limited to Windows environment
Quantum Numbers Corp	Quantum Cryptography	Quantum Random Number Generator (QRNG), high-speed encryption	Quantum-secure random number generation	Impossible to decipher random numbers	Still emerging technology

Tool Name	Type	Key Features	Use Cases	Advantages	Disadvantages
Homo-morphic Encryption	Advanced Encryption	Enables computations on encrypted data	Secure data processing without decryption	Stronger security for sensitive tasks	Limited functionality for all computations
AxCrypt Premium	Symmetric Encryption	128-bit and 256-bit AES encryption, cloud integration	Small business file encryption	Mobile app support	Free version lacks advanced features
Key-Based Authentication	Asymmetric Cryptography	Public/private keys for user authentication	Secure login systems	Eliminates password vulnerabilities	Requires careful key management

The table 4.2 summarizes various cryptographic tools based on their type, features, applications, advantages, and limitations.

Command-line utilities, such as OpenSSL, provide a versatile set of cryptographic functions that can be used for encryption, decryption, key generation, and certificate management. These utilities are often used by developers and system administrators to integrate cryptographic functionality into their applications and systems. OpenSSL, in particular, is a widely used open-source toolkit that supports a wide range of cryptographic algorithms and protocols.

Cryptographic libraries, such as Bouncy Castle and Crypto++, offer a collection of pre-built cryptographic functions that can be easily integrated into software applications. These libraries provide a higher level of abstraction than command-line utilities, making it easier for developers to implement secure communication and data protection. Cryptographic libraries typically support a wide range of programming languages and platforms.

Hardware Security Modules (HSMs) are physical devices that provide secure storage and management of cryptographic keys. HSMs are designed to resist tampering and protect keys from unauthorized access. They are often used in high-security environments, such as certificate authorities and financial institutions, to protect sensitive cryptographic keys.

Password managers are software applications that securely store and manage user passwords. These tools typically use strong encryption to protect passwords from unauthorized access, and they can generate strong, unique passwords for each website or application. Password managers can significantly improve user security by reducing the risk of password reuse and password cracking.

Digital signature tools enable users to create and verify digital signatures, ensuring the authenticity and integrity of electronic documents. These tools typically use asymmetric-key cryptography to create a digital signature that is unique to the signer and the document. Digital signatures are widely used for electronic contracts, software distribution, and other applications where authenticity and integrity are paramount.

4.5 ATTACKS ON CRYPTOSYSTEMS

Attacks on cryptosystems aim to break the security of cryptographic algorithms and protocols, revealing the underlying plaintext or compromising the cryptographic keys. These attacks exploit weaknesses in the algorithm, implementation, or key management practices. Understanding the different types of attacks is crucial for designing robust cryptosystems and mitigating potential vulnerabilities.

Brute-force attacks as given in figure 4.2 attempt to try every possible key until the correct one is found. The effectiveness of a brute-force attack depends on the key size and the computational resources available to the attacker. A key space of 2^{128} or higher is generally considered resistant to brute-force attacks with current technology.

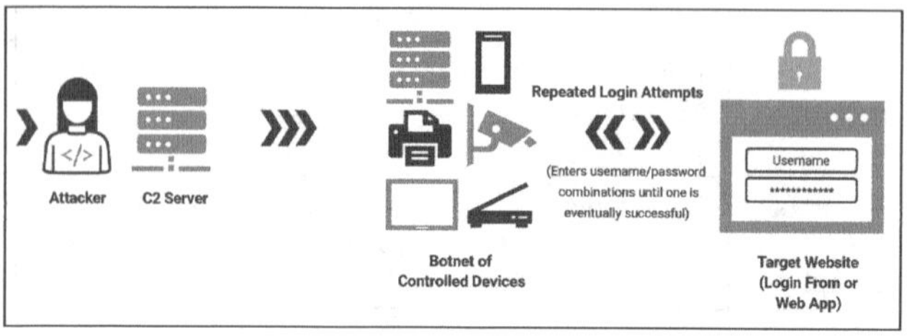

Figure 4.2: *How a BOTNET Brute Force Attack Works*

Cryptanalytic attacks exploit weaknesses in the cryptographic algorithm to deduce the key or recover the plaintext. These attacks often involve complex mathematical techniques and require a deep understanding of the algorithm's inner workings. Examples of cryptanalytic attacks include differential cryptanalysis, linear cryptanalysis, and side-channel attacks.

Implementation attacks target vulnerabilities in the software or hardware implementation of the cryptosystem. These attacks can exploit buffer overflows, timing variations, or power consumption patterns to extract cryptographic keys or bypass security controls. Secure coding practices and hardware security modules can help mitigate implementation attacks.

Social engineering attacks rely on manipulating individuals into revealing cryptographic keys or other sensitive information. These attacks can involve phishing emails, phone scams, or impersonating trusted individuals. User education and awareness training are essential for preventing social engineering attacks.

Side-channel attacks as in figure 4.3 exploit information leaked during the execution of a cryptographic algorithm, such as timing variations, power consumption, or electromagnetic radiation. By analyzing this information, an attacker can deduce the cryptographic key or recover the plaintext. Countermeasures against side-channel attacks include constant-time algorithms, power analysis countermeasures, and electromagnetic shielding.

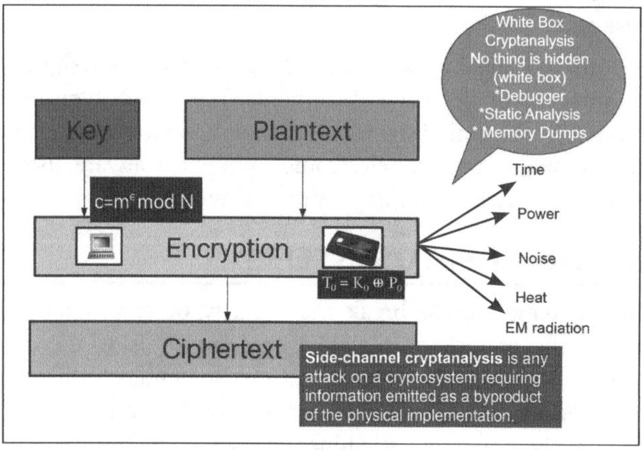

Figure 4.3: *Side Channel Attacks*

4.6 PHYSICAL SECURITY

Physical security refers to the measures taken to protect cryptographic systems and keys from physical threats, such as theft, tampering, and unauthorized access. These measures are essential for maintaining the confidentiality and integrity of cryptographic systems, especially in environments where physical access cannot be completely controlled.

Secure facilities are designed to protect cryptographic systems from physical threats. These facilities typically include controlled access, surveillance systems, and environmental controls. Access control measures can include biometric scanners, keycard systems, and security guards. Surveillance systems can monitor for unauthorized entry or suspicious activity. Environmental controls can protect against temperature extremes, humidity, and power outages.

Tamper-evident seals are used to detect unauthorized tampering with cryptographic devices or containers. These seals are designed to break or show signs of tampering if someone attempts to open or access the device. Tamper-evident seals can provide an additional layer of security, especially during transport or storage.

Secure storage devices, such as hardware security modules (HSMs), provide secure storage for cryptographic keys. These devices are designed to resist tampering and protect keys from unauthorized access. HSMs are often used in certificate authorities, financial institutions, and other high-security environments.

Background checks are performed to verify the trustworthiness and reliability of individuals who have access to cryptographic systems or keys. These checks can include criminal history checks, credit checks, and reference checks. Background checks can help prevent insider threats and ensure that only trusted individuals have access to sensitive cryptographic resources.

Destruction of cryptographic keys and systems is essential when they are no longer needed or when they have been compromised. Secure destruction methods can include shredding, burning, or degaussing. Proper destruction ensures that cryptographic keys and systems cannot be recovered and used for unauthorized purposes.

Video Resources

https://www.youtube.com/watch?v=GSIDS_lvRv4

Use of ICT

ICT is fundamentally interwoven with all aspects of modern cryptography, impacting everything from defining and disseminating cryptology terminology through online educational resources, to enabling the design and implementation of complex cipher methods and cryptographic algorithms using advanced programming languages and high-performance computing. Cryptographic tools, essential for secure communication and data protection, are almost entirely ICT-based, providing functionalities like encryption, decryption, and key management via software and hardware solutions. Simultaneously, ICT is leveraged in attacks on cryptosystems, utilizing powerful computing resources to break ciphers and exploit vulnerabilities, while conversely also powering the defensive measures like intrusion detection and prevention systems. Even in the realm of physical security, ICT plays a vital role through access control systems, surveillance technologies, and remote monitoring solutions, ensuring the protection of cryptographic keys and systems against unauthorized physical access and tampering. Therefore, ICT serves as both the enabler and the battleground for modern cryptography and security.

SUMMARY

- Cryptography secures data using ciphers, algorithms, and keys to ensure confidentiality.
- Various cipher methods, like substitution and transposition, offer different levels of security.
- Cryptographic algorithms, such as AES and RSA, encrypt and decrypt data using mathematical functions.
- Cryptographic tools, including OpenSSL and HSMs, facilitate the implementation and management of cryptographic functions.
- Attacks on cryptosystems, like brute-force and cryptanalysis, exploit weaknesses to compromise security.
- Physical security protects cryptographic systems and keys from physical threats and unauthorized access.

EXERCISES

A. Subjective Questions

Category-I **(Revised Bloom's Level - 1, 2 & 3): Knowledge, Comprehension, Application**

1. Define the terms "encryption" and "decryption" and explain their relationship. (Level 1, Knowledge)
2. Describe the difference between a substitution cipher and a transposition cipher. Give an example of each. (Level 2, Comprehension; Level 3, Application)
3. Explain how symmetric-key cryptography differs from asymmetric-key cryptography. (Level 2, Comprehension)
4. Outline three different uses for cryptographic hash functions. (Level 2, Comprehension)
5. Describe a common type of attack on cryptosystems and how it works. (Level 1, Knowledge; Level 2, Comprehension)
6. Explain why physical security is important in protecting cryptographic systems. (Level 2, Comprehension)

Category-II **(Revised Bloom's Level - 4, 5 & 6): Analysis, Synthesis, Evaluation**

1. Analyze the trade-offs between using symmetric and asymmetric encryption for a secure communication channel. (Level 4, Analysis)
2. Design a system for securely storing passwords that incorporates hashing and salting. (Level 6, Create)
3. Evaluate the effectiveness of different countermeasures against brute-force attacks on cryptosystems. (Level 5, Evaluate)
4. Given a scenario where a company's cryptographic keys have been compromised, analyze the likely security gaps and recommend improvements. (Level 4, Analysis; Level 6, Create)

5. Compare and contrast the security implications of using a weak cryptographic algorithm versus a strong one. (Level 5, Evaluate)
6. How does end-to-end encryption affect the role of third party services like email providers, and what are the implications for user privacy and data control? (Level 4, Analysis)

B. Objective Questions

Category-I (Revised Bloom's Level - 1, 2 & 3): Knowledge, Comprehension, Application

1. What is the purpose of encryption? (Level 1, Knowledge)
   (a) To hide the existence of a message (b) To compress data
   (c) To convert plaintext to ciphertext (d) To verify data integrity
2. A Caesar cipher is an example of what type of cipher? (Level 1, Knowledge)
   (a) Transposition cipher (b) Substitution cipher
   (c) Block cipher (d) Stream cipher
3. Which type of cryptography uses a single key for both encryption and decryption? (Level 1, Knowledge)
   (a) Asymmetric-key cryptography (b) Symmetric-key cryptography
   (c) Hashing (d) Steganography
4. Which of the following is a common use for cryptographic hash functions? (Level 2, Comprehension)
   (a) Encrypting data (b) Generating random numbers
   (c) Verifying data integrity (d) Securing network connections
5. A brute-force attack attempts to: (Level 2, Comprehension)
   (a) Exploit weaknesses in a cryptographic algorithm
   (b) Guess the correct key by trying all possibilities
   (c) Manipulate users into revealing their passwords
   (d) Intercept network traffic
6. Storing cryptographic keys in a Hardware Security Module (HSM) primarily addresses which security concern? (Level 2, Comprehension)
   (a) Availability (b) Confidentiality
   (c) Integrity (d) Non-repudiation

Category-II (Revised Bloom's Level - 4, 5 & 6): Analysis, Synthesis, Evaluation

1. Which of the following scenarios would BEST justify the use of asymmetric-key cryptography over symmetric-key cryptography? (Level 5, Evaluate)
   (a) Encrypting large amounts of data for storage
   (b) Securing a real-time video conference
   (c) Exchanging a secret key securely over the internet
   (d) Hashing passwords for storage

2. A company wants to implement a password storage system that protects against rainbow table attacks. Which of the following is the MOST suitable choice? (Level 5, Evaluate)
   (a) Storing passwords in plaintext
   (b) Hashing passwords with a weak algorithm
   (c) Hashing passwords with a strong algorithm and a unique salt
   (d) Encrypting passwords with a symmetric key
3. Which of the following physical security measures BEST addresses the risk of unauthorized access to a server room? (Level 5, Evaluate)
   (a) Installing brighter lights in the server room
   (b) Implementing multi-factor authentication (MFA)
   (c) Leaving the server room door unlocked for easy access
   (d) Posting security policies on the server room door
4. An organization has implemented strong encryption for data at rest and in transit. What additional security measure would MOST enhance their ability to detect and respond to data breaches? (Level 5, Evaluate)
   (a) Data Loss Prevention (DLP) system
   (b) Intrusion Detection System (IDS)
   (c) Vulnerability Scanner
   (d) Password Manager
5. An organization needs to balance strong cryptographic security with ease of use for its employees. Which approach BEST achieves this balance for encrypting email communications? (Level 6, Evaluate)
   (a) Requiring employees to manually encrypt and decrypt every email
   (b) Implementing a transparent email encryption solution that automatically encrypts and decrypts emails
   (c) Disabling email encryption entirely
   (d) Allowing unrestricted email access with no security measures
6. What are the implications of quantum computing for modern cryptographic algorithms like RSA and ECC, and what strategies can be employed to mitigate these risks? (Level 4, Analysis)

TEACHER'S KNOW MORE

Teachers should be familiar with cryptology terminology (like encryption, decryption, ciphers, keys), understand different cipher methods (substitution, transposition), and be able to explain common cryptographic algorithms (AES, RSA) and tools (hash functions, digital signatures). It's important to discuss common attacks on cryptosystems (brute force, dictionary attacks, man-in-the-middle attacks) and the importance of key management. Finally, they must stress that physical security (access controls, surveillance, environmental protection) is a vital, often overlooked, component of overall security, complementing cryptographic measures by protecting the physical infrastructure that houses sensitive data and systems.

5 UNIT Protocols for Secure Communication

RATIONALE

A dedicated book chapter on Protocols for Secure Communication is essential for a comprehensive understanding of cybersecurity, as it bridges the gap between cryptographic principles and their practical application in securing data transmission across networks. Covering basic concepts establishes a foundation for understanding protocol design and functionality. An examination of protocols like SHTTP, SSL/TLS, and SET illuminates the evolution of secure web communication. Exploring S/MIME, PEM, and PGP provides insights into secure email practices. Addressing WEP, WPA, and WPA2 highlights the vulnerabilities and advancements in wireless security. Finally, a discussion of IPSec demonstrates how secure communication can be established at the network layer. By analyzing these protocols, the chapter provides critical insights into how secure communication is achieved in diverse environments, from web browsing to email exchange, wireless networks, and virtual private networks, thus equipping readers with the knowledge to evaluate, implement, and troubleshoot secure communication systems.

UNIT OUTCOMES

- **Understand Secure Communication Protocols:** Students will be able to define and differentiate between SHTTP, SSL, and SET protocols for secure web transactions.
- **Compare Email Security Standards:** Students will be able to compare and contrast S/MIME, PEM, and PGP for secure email communication, explaining their key features and applications.
- **Analyze Wireless Security Protocols:** Students will be able to analyze the evolution of wireless security protocols, including WEP, WPA, and WPA2, highlighting their strengths and weaknesses.
- **Describe VPN Security Solutions:** Students will be able to describe IPSEC for creating secure VPN connections and explain how it ensures confidentiality, integrity, and authenticity.
- **Apply Encryption Tools:** Students will be able to explain how tools like PGP are used to ensure data security.

5.1 BASIC CONCEPTS OF SECURE COMMUNICATION

Secure communication is the process of transmitting information in a way that protects it from unauthorized access, modification, or disclosure. It is a cornerstone of modern cybersecurity, ensuring privacy, integrity, and authenticity in various digital interactions. At its heart, secure communication relies on cryptography, the science of encoding and decoding messages to keep them secret. However, cryptography alone is not enough; a secure communication system also requires robust protocols, key management practices, and authentication mechanisms.

Several fundamental concepts underpin secure communication. Confidentiality ensures that only authorized parties can access the transmitted information. Integrity guarantees that the message remains unaltered during transit, preventing tampering or corruption. Authentication verifies the identity of the sender and receiver, ensuring that communication occurs between trusted parties. Non-repudiation provides proof that a message was sent and received, preventing either party from denying their involvement.

Protocols are essential for establishing secure communication channels. They define the rules and procedures for exchanging information, including how to encrypt and decrypt messages, authenticate users, and manage cryptographic keys. Secure protocols often incorporate cryptographic algorithms, hash functions, and digital signatures to achieve confidentiality, integrity, and authentication. Common examples include Transport Layer Security (TLS) for securing web traffic and Secure Shell (SSH) for remote access.

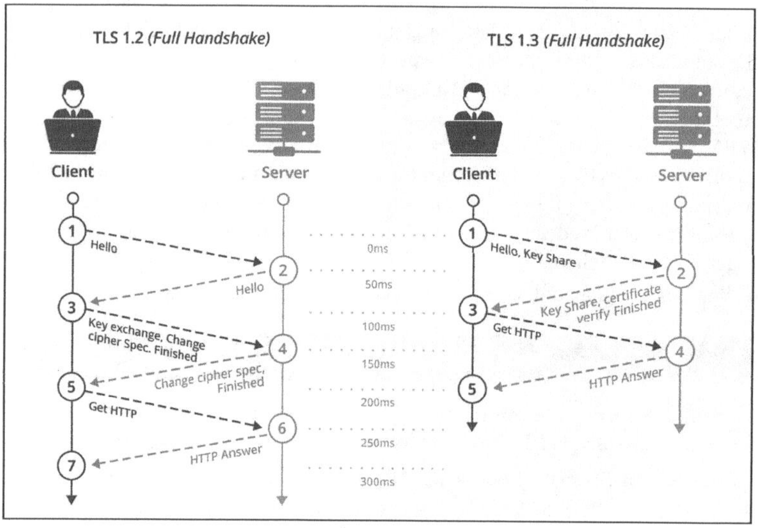

Figure 5.1: *TLS*

The figure 5.1 visually compares the full handshake process for establishing a secure connection using TLS (Transport Layer Security) versions 1.2 and 1.3. On both sides, it shows the communication flow between a client and a server. The process begins similarly for both versions with the client sending a "Hello" message to the server, initiating the connection. This "Hello" includes information about the client's supported cryptographic algorithms and TLS version. The server responds with its own "Hello" message, selecting the cryptographic parameters for the session.

The major differences become apparent in the subsequent steps. In TLS 1.2, there's a separate key exchange phase, followed by the "Change Cipher Spec" message which signals the start of encrypted communication. The server then sends a "Finished" message, indicating that it has completed the handshake. After that, the client sends its own "Change Cipher Spec" and "Finished" messages. Only after all these steps, both client and server can exchange application data (e.g., "Get HTTP" and "HTTP Answer").

TLS 1.3 streamlines this process for improved efficiency and security. Key exchange is incorporated directly into the initial "Hello" messages, reducing the number of round trips needed. The "Change Cipher Spec" message is eliminated, and the "Finished" messages are sent earlier in the process, before the actual HTTP request and response. By reducing the number of steps and integrating key exchange, TLS 1.3 achieves faster connection establishment and enhances security by removing support for weaker cryptographic algorithms supported in older versions. The diagram clearly illustrates these differences, highlighting the efficiency and security improvements introduced in TLS 1.3.

Transport Layer Security (TLS) is a cryptographic protocol designed to ensure secure communication over the internet by providing privacy, data integrity, and authentication. It operates primarily at the transport layer of the OSI model and is widely used to encrypt application-layer protocols such as HTTP, SMTP, and VoIP. TLS establishes a secure connection through a handshake process, which involves negotiating encryption algorithms, exchanging keys using public key cryptography, and authenticating the server's identity via digital certificates. Once the handshake is complete, the session key enables encrypted data transfer between client and server. TLS safeguards against threats like message tampering, interception, and forgery, making it essential for secure web applications, email communication, and e-commerce.

Secure Shell (SSH) as given in figure 5.2 is a cryptographic network protocol designed to securely access and manage remote systems over an unsecured network. It replaces older, insecure protocols like Telnet and FTP by providing encrypted communication, strong authentication (password or public-key-based), and data integrity. SSH operates on a client-server model, where the client initiates a connection to the server, typically on TCP port 22. During the connection setup, the protocol negotiates encryption algorithms, exchanges keys, and establishes a secure channel for data transfer. SSH is widely used for remote login, file transfers, and administrative tasks, offering features like port forwarding (tunneling) and secure command execution. Its robust encryption ensures that transmitted data remains confidential and protected from eavesdropping or tampering, making it essential for managing servers, infrastructure, and sensitive network operations.

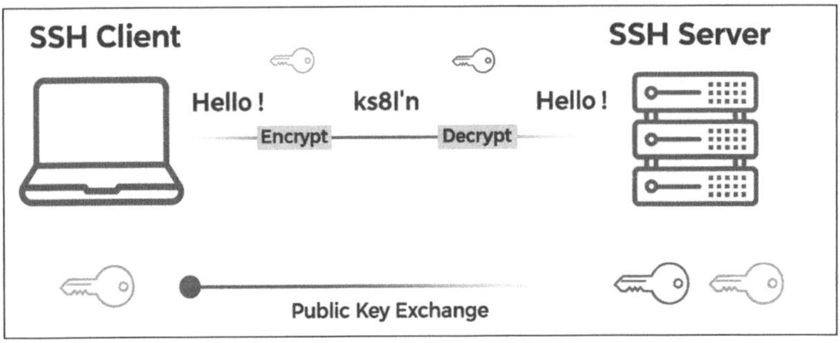

Figure 5.2: *SSH*

Key management is a critical aspect of secure communication, involving the generation, storage, distribution, and revocation of cryptographic keys. Secure key management practices are essential to prevent unauthorized access to keys, which could compromise the entire communication system. Key exchange protocols, such as Diffie-Hellman, enable parties to securely establish a shared secret key over an insecure channel. Public Key Infrastructure (PKI) provides a framework for managing digital certificates, which are used to verify the identity of users and devices.

The security of any communication system depends on the strength of its weakest link. Vulnerabilities in protocols, weak cryptographic algorithms, poor key management practices, or inadequate authentication mechanisms can all compromise security. Regular security audits, penetration testing, and vulnerability assessments are essential to identify and address potential weaknesses. Staying informed about the latest threats and security best practices is crucial for maintaining secure communication in an evolving threat landscape.

5.2 SHTTP, SSL & SET

SHTTP (Secure Hypertext Transfer Protocol) as given in figure 5.3 was an early attempt to secure web communications by extending the basic HTTP protocol. It allowed for the encryption of individual messages, offering flexibility in securing specific parts of a transaction rather than the entire connection. SHTTP supported multiple encryption algorithms and key exchange methods, allowing users to choose the level of security appropriate for their needs. However, SHTTP was less widely adopted than SSL, and its development has largely been superseded by more comprehensive security protocols.

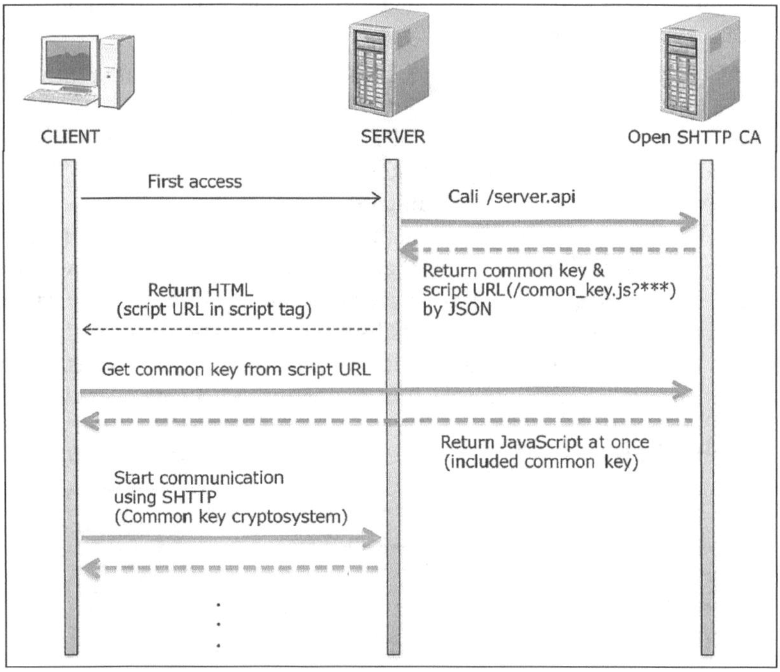

Figure 5.3: *Secure Hyper Text Transfer Protocol*

SSL (Secure Sockets Layer), and its successor TLS (Transport Layer Security), is a widely used protocol for establishing secure connections between a web server and a browser. SSL/TLS operates at the transport layer, providing encryption, authentication, and data integrity for all traffic between the client and server. When a user accesses a website with SSL/TLS enabled, the browser and server negotiate a secure connection using cryptographic algorithms and digital certificates.

The SSL/TLS handshake process involves several steps, including key exchange, authentication, and cipher suite negotiation. The client and server exchange cryptographic keys using either symmetric or asymmetric encryption. The server presents a digital certificate, which is verified by the client to ensure the server's identity. The client and server then negotiate a cipher suite, which specifies the encryption algorithm, hash function, and key exchange method to be used for the session.

SSL/TLS has evolved over time to address security vulnerabilities and improve performance. Newer versions of TLS, such as TLS 1.3, offer enhanced security features, including stronger encryption algorithms, improved key exchange methods, and reduced latency. However, older versions of SSL and TLS are vulnerable to attacks and should be disabled. It is important to keep SSL/TLS implementations up-to-date with the latest security patches and best practices.

SET (Secure Electronic Transaction) as given in figure 5.4 was a protocol developed by Visa and Mastercard to secure credit card transactions over the internet. SET used digital certificates and cryptography to protect sensitive payment information, such as credit card numbers and expiration dates. The SET protocol involved multiple parties, including the cardholder, merchant, payment gateway, and certificate authority. However, SET was complex to implement and never achieved widespread adoption. It has largely been replaced by simpler, more flexible solutions for securing online payments.

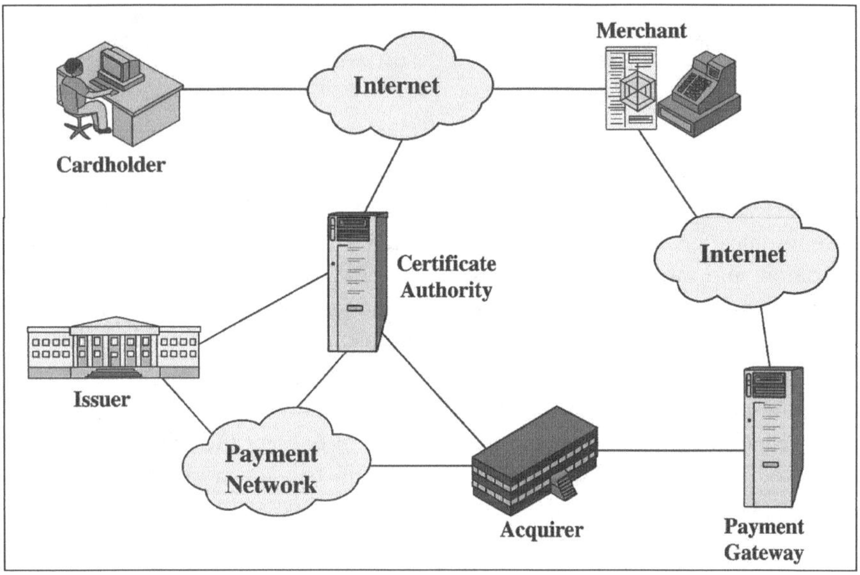

Figure 5.4: *Participants in the SET System*

5.3 S/MIME, PEM & PGP

S/MIME (Secure/Multipurpose Internet Mail Extensions) as given in figure 5.5 is a standard for encrypting and digitally signing email messages. It provides confidentiality, integrity, authentication, and non-repudiation for email communication. S/MIME uses public-key cryptography to encrypt email messages, ensuring that only the intended recipient can decrypt and read them. It also uses digital signatures to verify the sender's identity and ensure that the message has not been tampered with.

S/MIME relies on X.509 digital certificates to verify the identity of email users and to manage cryptographic keys. Users obtain digital certificates from a trusted certificate authority (CA), which verifies their identity and issues a certificate containing their public key. When sending an S/MIME-protected email, the sender's digital signature is attached to the message, allowing the recipient to verify the sender's identity and the integrity of the message.

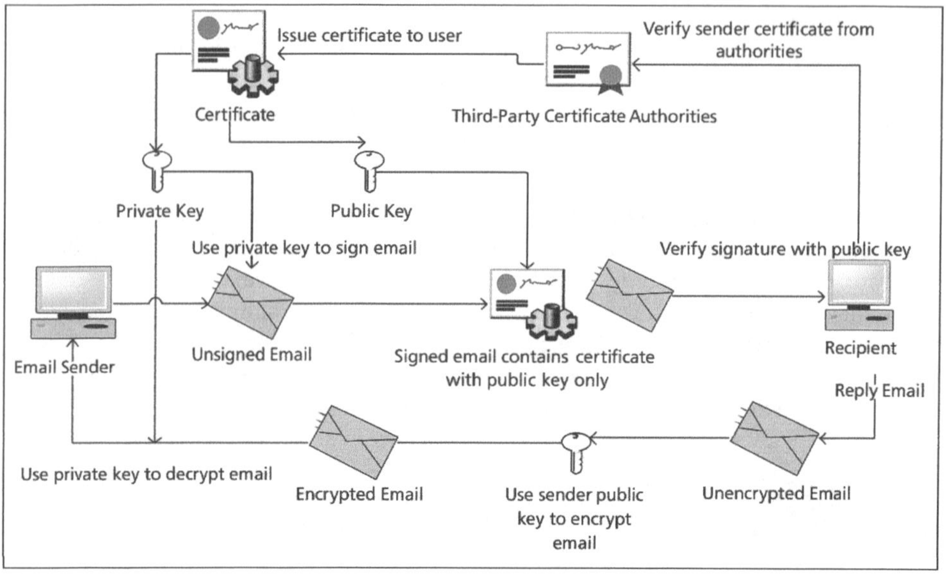

Figure 5.5: *S/MIME Structure*

PEM (Privacy Enhanced Mail) as given in figure 5.6 was an early standard for securing email communications. PEM used cryptographic techniques to provide confidentiality, authentication, and integrity for email messages. PEM was designed to be interoperable with existing email systems, but it required modifications to email clients and servers. PEM never achieved widespread adoption due to its complexity and lack of vendor support.

PGP (Pretty Good Privacy) is a widely used encryption program that provides cryptographic privacy and authentication for data communication. PGP is often used to encrypt email messages, but it can also be used to encrypt files, disk partitions, and other types of data. PGP uses a combination of symmetric-key cryptography, public-key cryptography, and hashing to provide a high level of security.

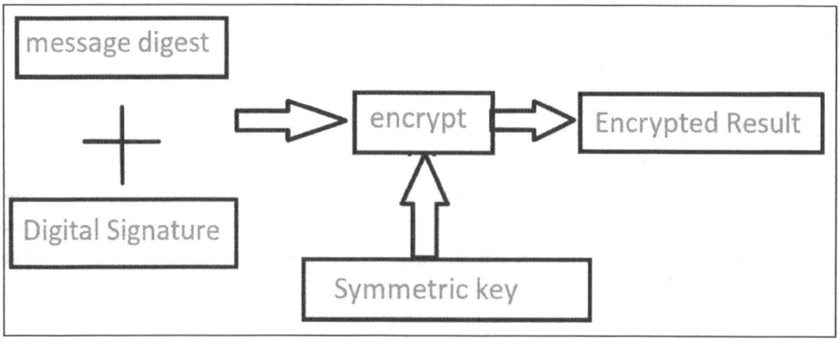

Figure 5.6: *PEM*

PGP as given in figure 5.7 is based on a web of trust model, where users digitally sign each other's public keys to establish trust. This allows users to verify the authenticity of public keys without relying on a central certificate authority. PGP is available for a variety of operating systems and is supported by many email clients and other applications. It remains a popular choice for individuals and organizations who need to protect the privacy and security of their data.

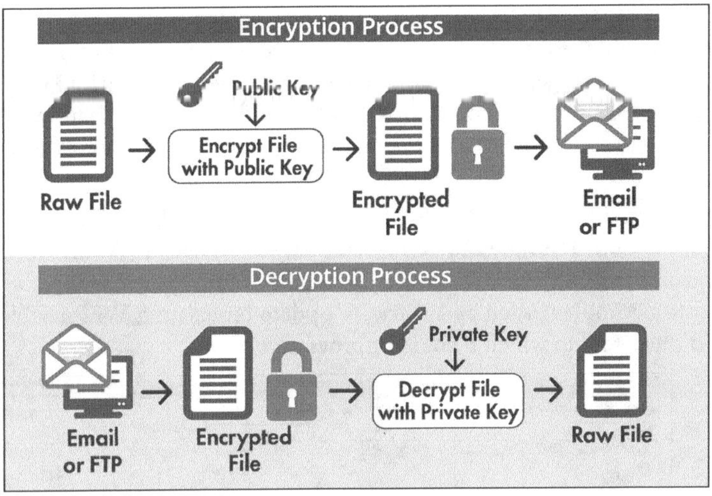

Figure 5.7: PGP

5.4 WEP, WPA & WPA2

WEP (Wired Equivalent Privacy) as represented in figure 5.8 was one of the first security protocols developed to secure wireless networks. It aimed to provide the same level of security as a wired network by encrypting data transmitted over the airwaves. WEP used the RC4 stream cipher for encryption and a 24-bit initialization vector (IV) to vary the encryption key. However, WEP was quickly found to have serious security vulnerabilities.

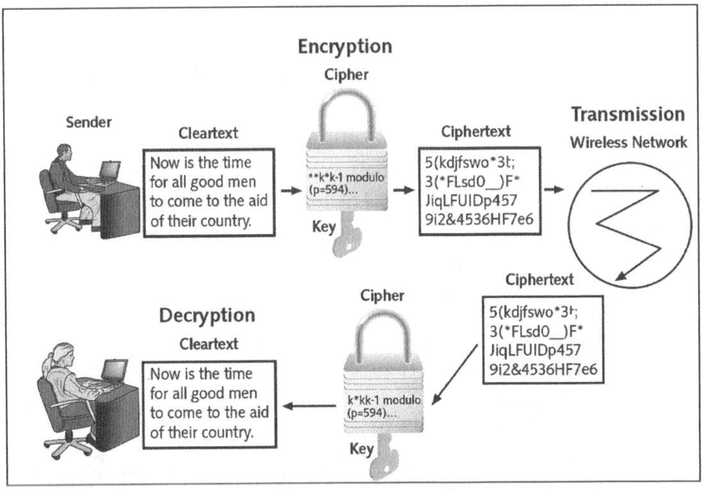

Figure 5.8: WEP

The WEP protocol used a shared key that was the same for all users on the network. The short IV and the way it was used in the RC4 algorithm made it relatively easy for attackers to capture enough data to crack the WEP key. Tools were developed that automated the process of cracking WEP keys in a matter of minutes. As a result, WEP was quickly deprecated and replaced by stronger security protocols.

WPA (Wi-Fi Protected Access) was developed as an interim solution to address the security vulnerabilities in WEP. WPA introduced several improvements over WEP, including a new key management protocol called Temporal Key Integrity Protocol (TKIP) and a stronger message integrity check (MIC) called Michael. TKIP dynamically generated new encryption keys for each packet, making it much more difficult for attackers to crack the WPA key.

WPA also included support for 802.1X authentication, which allowed for stronger authentication methods than the shared key authentication used by WEP. However, WPA was still based on the RC4 cipher, which was eventually found to have vulnerabilities. WPA was designed to be implemented as a software update on existing WEP-enabled devices, which limited the extent to which it could improve security.

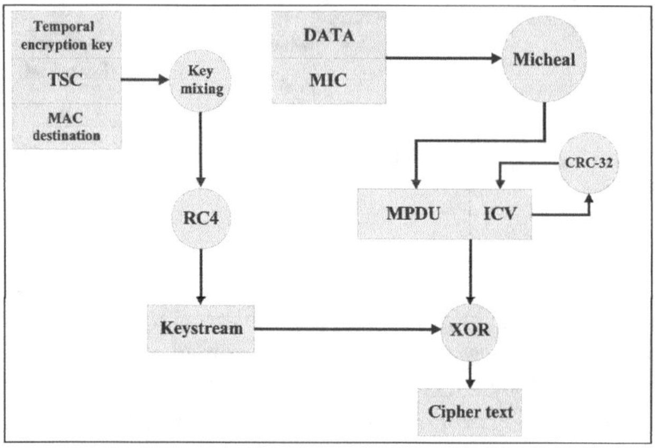

***Figure 5.9:** WPA Encryption Process*

The figure 5.9 illustrates the encryption process used in WPA (Wi-Fi Protected Access), specifically its implementation with the Temporal Key Integrity Protocol (TKIP). The process begins with key mixing, where a **Temporal Encryption Key**, the **TSC (Temporal Sequence Counter)**, and the **MAC destination address** are combined to generate a per-packet key. This ensures that every packet is encrypted with a unique key, significantly improving security by preventing key reuse. The mixed key is then passed to the RC4 stream cipher, which generates a keystream used for encryption. RC4 is a symmetric stream cipher that combines the keystream with plaintext data to produce ciphertext.

On the data side, WPA includes mechanisms for maintaining data integrity. The plaintext data is first processed by a Message Integrity Code (MIC) algorithm called "Michael," which generates a MIC value to protect against tampering. This MIC is appended to the data, forming the MPDU (MAC Protocol Data Unit). To further ensure integrity, a CRC-32 (Cyclic Redundancy Check) is applied to the MPDU, producing an Integrity Check Value (ICV). The ICV helps detect errors or modifications in transit. The resulting MPDU and ICV are combined and prepared for encryption.

Finally, the RC4-generated keystream and the prepared MPDU/ICV combination are XORed together to produce the final ciphertext. This ciphertext is transmitted over the wireless network. The use of XOR ensures that the data cannot be decrypted without access to both the keystream and the original encryption key. By combining encryption (via RC4) and integrity mechanisms (MIC and CRC-32), WPA provides both confidentiality and protection against tampering. However, while it was an improvement over WEP, WPA's reliance on RC4 and certain vulnerabilities in MIC led to its eventual replacement by WPA2 with stronger encryption protocols like AES-CCMP.

WPA2 (Wi-Fi Protected Access 2) is the successor to WPA and provides significantly stronger security. WPA2 uses the Advanced Encryption Standard (AES) with Counter Mode with Cipher Block Chaining Message Authentication Code Protocol (CCMP) for encryption, which is much more secure than the RC4 cipher used by WEP and WPA. WPA2 also supports 802.1X authentication and provides improved key management and message integrity. WPA2 is the recommended security protocol for most wireless networks today.

Wi-Fi Protected Access 2 (WPA2) is a security protocol developed by the Wi-Fi Alliance and ratified in 2004 as part of the IEEE 802.11i standard. It replaced WPA by introducing stronger encryption and authentication mechanisms to secure wireless networks. WPA2 uses the Advanced Encryption Standard (AES) for encryption and the Counter Mode with Cipher Block Chaining Message Authentication Code Protocol (CCMP) for data integrity and confidentiality. These features ensure that only authorized users can access the network and that transmitted data remains protected against tampering or interception. WPA2 operates in two modes: Personal mode, which uses a pre-shared key (PSK) for home and small office networks, and Enterprise mode, which employs Extensible Authentication Protocol (EAP) for larger organizations requiring centralized authentication.

Despite its robust security, WPA2 is not without vulnerabilities. The KRACK (Key Reinstallation Attack) vulnerability discovered in 2017 exposed flaws in the four-way handshake process used to establish secure connections, allowing attackers within range to potentially decrypt traffic. Additionally, WPA2 networks with weak passwords are susceptible to brute-force or dictionary attacks. To mitigate these risks, users are advised to use strong, complex passwords and ensure devices are updated with security patches. While WPA2 remains widely used due to its strong encryption, it has been succeeded by WPA3, which addresses these vulnerabilities and offers enhanced security features for modern wireless networks.

5.5 IPSEC & PGP

IPSec (Internet Protocol Security) is a suite of protocols that provides secure communication over IP networks. It offers confidentiality, integrity, and authentication at the network layer, protecting all traffic between two hosts or networks. IPSec is commonly used to create Virtual Private Networks (VPNs), securing communication between remote users and corporate networks, or between different branches of an organization.

IPSec operates in two main modes: **transport mode** and **tunnel mode.** In transport mode, IPSec protects the data payload of IP packets, while leaving the IP header unchanged. This mode is typically used for securing communication between two hosts on the same network. In tunnel mode, IPSec encrypts the entire IP packet, including the header, and encapsulates it within a new IP packet. This mode is used to create VPNs, securing communication between two networks over the internet.

IPSec uses two main protocols to provide security: **Authentication Header (AH)** and **Encapsulating Security Payload (ESP).** AH provides authentication and integrity, ensuring that the packet has not been tampered with and that it originates from a trusted source. ESP provides confidentiality, encrypting the data payload to prevent unauthorized access. ESP can also provide authentication and integrity, if configured to do so. The working of IPSec is as represented in figure 5.10.

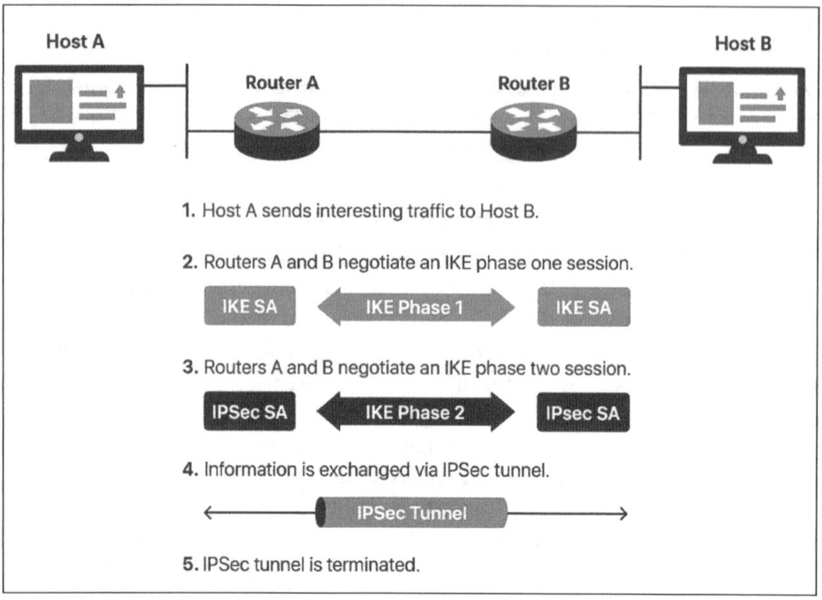

Figure 5.10: *Working of IPSec*

Internet Protocol Security (IPsec) is a suite of protocols designed to provide secure communication over IP networks by ensuring data confidentiality, integrity, and authentication. Operating at the network layer (OSI Layer 3), IPsec secures data flows between hosts, gateways, or a combination of both. It achieves this through two main protocols: the Authentication Header (AH), which provides data integrity and source authentication, and the Encapsulating Security Payload (ESP), which ensures encryption and optional authentication. IPsec supports two modes of operation: transport mode, which encrypts only the payload of the IP packet, and tunnel mode, which encrypts the entire packet and encapsulates it with a new IP header. These features make IPsec widely used for Virtual Private Networks (VPNs), enabling secure communication over public networks like the internet.

IPsec relies on cryptographic techniques such as symmetric encryption, public-key cryptography, and hashing to protect against threats like eavesdropping, replay attacks, and data tampering. The Internet Key Exchange (IKE) protocol is used to establish Security Associations (SAs), which define the cryptographic parameters for secure communication. IPsec's flexibility allows it to work with both IPv4 and IPv6 networks, making it suitable for modern network infrastructures. Its applications range from securing site-to-site VPNs for businesses to protecting individual device communications. However, due to its complexity and configuration requirements, IPsec can be challenging to implement and maintain effectively in some environments. Despite this, its robust security features make it a cornerstone of network security solutions.

PGP (Pretty Good Privacy) provides cryptographic privacy and authentication for data communication. PGP uses a combination of symmetric-key cryptography, public-key cryptography, and hashing to provide a high level of security. It allows users to encrypt and digitally sign emails, files, and other types of data, protecting them from unauthorized access and tampering.

While IPSec operates at the network layer, securing all traffic between two points, PGP typically operates at the application layer, securing specific messages or files. IPSec is often used to create secure tunnels between networks, while PGP is used to protect individual pieces of data. Both IPSec and PGP play important roles in securing communication in different contexts. They can even be used in conjunction, with PGP securing the data payload and IPSec securing the network connection.

Video Resources

- Cryptography: Crash Course Computer Science #33:
  https://www.youtube.com/watch?v=jhXCtBwFNmA
- How does SSL work? - Computerphile:
  https://www.youtube.com/watch?v=SsqvFg3gOZ8
- PGP Encryption: https://www.youtube.com/watch?v=QrjRvgjwTvU
- Cracking WEP with Kali Linux:
  https://www.youtube.com/watch?v=wVu7o13MQu4
- What is IPsec? VPN Technologies Explained:
  https://www.youtube.com/watch?v=mQYT5kS82aw

Use of ICT

ICT is essential to the implementation, management, and evolution of secure communication protocols. For basic concepts, ICT provides the platforms for education, research, and collaboration needed to define and refine cryptographic principles. Regarding SHTTP, SSL & SET, ICT enables the software libraries, web servers, and browsers that implement these protocols, along with tools for vulnerability discovery and mitigation. In the realm of S/MIME, PEM, and PGP, ICT underpins the creation, distribution, and validation of digital certificates, and facilitates secure key exchange through online key servers and web-of-trust models. For wireless security protocols like WEP, WPA, and WPA2, ICT not only allows for their implementation in devices but also provides the analytical tools necessary to uncover vulnerabilities and develop stronger protocols. Finally, with IPSEC & PGP, ICT again plays a dual role, supporting the creation and deployment of these protocols, as well as the analytical tools used to identify and address potential weaknesses, ensuring ongoing security and reliability.

SUMMARY

- **Secure communication protocols** (like SSL/TLS, IPsec) are vital for protecting data confidentiality, integrity, and authenticity during transmission across networks.
- **Various protocols address different layers** (application, transport, network) and communication types (web, email, VPNs), each with unique security mechanisms.
- **Encryption, authentication, and key management** are core components ensuring secure channels.
- **WEP has been deprecated** due to vulnerabilities, replaced by stronger protocols like WPA2/3 for wireless security.
- **Understanding the strengths and weaknesses** of different protocols is crucial for selecting the appropriate solution based on security requirements and context.

EXERCISES

A. Subjective Questions

Category-I (Revised Bloom's Level - 1, 2 & 3): Knowledge, Comprehension, Application

1. Define what a secure communication protocol is, and explain its primary purpose. (Level 1, Knowledge)
2. Describe the difference between SHTTP and SSL/TLS. What specific problem did SSL/TLS solve better? (Level 2, Comprehension)
3. Explain how digital certificates are used in SSL/TLS to establish a secure connection. (Level 2, Comprehension)
4. Outline three ways that S/MIME enhances the security of email communications. (Level 2, Comprehension)
5. Describe the weaknesses of WEP and explain how WPA and WPA2 addressed those weaknesses. (Level 2, Comprehension)
6. Explain how IPSec can be used to create a Virtual Private Network (VPN). (Level 2 & 3, Comprehension and Application)

Category-II (Revised Bloom's Level - 4, 5 & 6): Analysis, Synthesis, Evaluation

1. Analyze the security trade-offs between using SSL/TLS with a strong cipher suite versus a weak cipher suite. (Level 4, Analysis)
2. Design a secure email system that incorporates S/MIME and addresses the challenges of key management. (Level 6, Create)
3. Evaluate the security of a Wi-Fi network using WPA2-PSK with a weak password, and propose improvements. (Level 5, Evaluate)
4. Given a scenario where a company needs to secure communication between its headquarters and branch offices, analyze the factors to consider when choosing between IPSec and SSL/TLS VPNs. (Level 4, Analysis)
5. Compare and contrast the security models of PGP and S/MIME for email encryption. Which is more suitable for different scenarios and why? (Level 5, Evaluate)
6. Analyze the potential impact of quantum computing on the security of widely used protocols like SSL/TLS, and discuss possible mitigation strategies. (Level 4, Analysis)

B. Objective Questions

Category-I (Revised Bloom's Level - 1, 2 & 3): Knowledge, Comprehension, Application

1. Which of the following protocols is commonly used to secure web traffic? (Level 1, Knowledge)

   (a) SHTTP (b) SSL/TLS
   (c) SET (d) PGP

2. What is the primary function of a digital certificate in SSL/TLS? (Level 1, Knowledge)
   (a) Encrypting data (b) Compressing data
   (c) Verifying the server's identity (d) Protecting against malware
3. S/MIME is primarily used for securing what type of communication? (Level 1, Knowledge)
   (a) Web browsing (b) Email
   (c) Wireless networks (d) VPNs
4. Which of the following was found to have significant security vulnerabilities? (Level 1, Knowledge)
   (a) WPA2 (b) WPA
   (c) WEP (d) IPSec
5. IPSec operates at which layer of the OSI model? (Level 2, Comprehension)
   (a) Application Layer (b) Transport Layer
   (c) Network Layer (d) Data Link Layer
6. Which of the following protocols can use the AES encryption algorithm? (Level 2, Comprehension)
   (a) WEP (b) WPA with TKIP
   (c) WPA2 (d) SSL 3.0

Category-II (Revised Bloom's Level - 4, 5 & 6): Analysis, Synthesis, Evaluation

1. A company wants to implement end-to-end encryption for its internal email communications. Which of the following options would be MOST suitable? (Level 5, Evaluate)
   (a) Using S/MIME with a centralized key management system
   (b) Using PGP with a decentralized web of trust
   (c) Using SSL/TLS for email server connections only
   (d) Storing email data in encrypted databases
2. Which of the following scenarios would BEST justify the use of IPsec tunnel mode? (Level 5, Evaluate)
   (a) Securing communication between a web server and a client
   (b) Securing communication between two hosts on the same local network
   (c) Creating a VPN between two branch offices
   (d) Encrypting individual email messages
3. An organization needs to deploy a secure wireless network with the strongest possible security. Which of the following configurations is the BEST choice? (Level 5, Evaluate)
   (a) WEP with a long passphrase
   (b) WPA with TKIP and a strong password
   (c) WPA2 with AES-CCMP and 802.1X authentication
   (d) Disabling wireless security entirely and relying on physical security

4. An attacker has successfully performed a man-in-the-middle attack on an SSL/TLS connection. Which of the following countermeasures would be MOST effective in preventing future attacks? (Level 5, Evaluate)
   (a) Implementing stronger encryption algorithms
   (b) Enforcing strict certificate validation and using HSTS (HTTP Strict Transport Security)
   (c) Regularly changing the server's private key
   (d) Blocking all traffic from suspicious IP addresses
5. A security consultant is asked to evaluate the effectiveness of a company's VPN solution. What aspect should they prioritize when evaluating the security of the VPN tunnel itself? (Level 6, Evaluate)
   (a) The number of users connected to the VPN
   (b) The physical location of the VPN server
   (c) The cryptographic algorithms and key exchange methods used by IPsec or SSL/TLS
   (d) The color scheme of the VPN client software
6. A company is migrating its infrastructure to the cloud and needs to secure communication between its on-premises network and its cloud resources. Which of the following approaches would be MOST suitable for establishing a secure connection? (Level 6, Evaluate)
   (a) Using a simple port forwarding configuration
   (b) Implementing a site-to-site VPN using IPsec
   (c) Relying on the cloud provider's built-in security features
   (d) Disabling all network traffic between on-premises and cloud environments

TEACHER'S KNOW MORE

To effectively teach secure communication protocols, instructors should emphasize that confidentiality, integrity, and availability, while fundamental, are insufficient without robust authentication and non-repudiation mechanisms, highlighting the layered approach required for true security. It is critical to present the evolution of protocols like SHTTP, SSL/TLS, SET, WEP, WPA, and WPA2 within their historical context, showcasing how each iteration addresses prior vulnerabilities and limitations, while also clarifying that some, like WEP and SET, are now largely obsolete. When discussing S/MIME, PEM, and PGP, underscore the importance of understanding the contrasting trust models – PKI versus Web of Trust – and the inherent key management challenges associated with each. For all protocols, instructors must move beyond simple definitions to explore implementation details, cipher suite negotiations, potential attack vectors, and the trade-offs between security and performance. Furthermore, teachers should highlight that strong passwords/passphrases are crucial and must always be used, and should include hands-on activities like packet analysis, ethical hacking exercises, and real-world case studies to demonstrate real-world application of the concepts while dispelling misconceptions like "encryption alone guarantees security" or "hiding the SSID makes a network secure". Instructors should continually stress the importance of staying current with emerging threats and protocol updates, as the landscape of secure communication is constantly evolving.